**Television
and the
Presidential
Elections**

Television and the Presidential Elections

Self-Interest and the Public Interest

Edited by
Martin Linsky
Harvard University

A Project of the Institute of
Politics, John F. Kennedy
School of Government,
Harvard University

Lexington Books
D.C. Heath and Company
Lexington, Massachusetts
Toronto

Library of Congress Cataloging in Publication Data
Main entry under title:

Television and the presidential elections.

   Based on a conference held at the Institute of Politics, John Fitzgerald
Kennedy School of Government, Cambridge, Mass., Jan. 29–31, 1982.
   Bibliography: p.
   1. Television in politics—United States—Congresses. 2. Presidents—
United States—Election—Congresses. I. Linsky, Martin. II. John
Fitzgerald Kennedy School of Government.
HE8700.7.P6T44   1983   324.7'3'0973   82-49010
ISBN 0-669-06397-5 (Casebound)
ISBN 0-669-06947-7 (Paperbound)

Copyright © 1983 by D.C. Heath and Company

Published simultaneously in Canada

Printed in the United States of America

Casebound International Standard Book Number: 0-669-06397-5

Paperbound International Standard Book Number: 0-669-06947-7

Library of Congress Catalog Card Number: 82-49010

To ABC, CBS, and NBC who made this conference and this book possible and significant, and to Alison, Sam, and Max who make it all worthwhile.

Contents

Acknowledgments

The Conference on Television and the Presidential Elections could not have been held and this book could not have been produced without the guidance and assistance of dozens of people who were involved at various stages from the beginnings of the idea to the completion of the manuscript. Many of them are included in the conference program, reprinted here in the appendix.

There are some, however, whose participation deserves special mention. Much of the early thinking about the conference came from the fertile mind of Tanya Melich, a fellow at the Institute of Politics in the spring of 1980 and on leave at that time from her position as director of civic affairs for CBS, Inc. The conference would never have taken place if there had not been one person at each of the three networks who was willing to take the financial, political, and intellectual leaps of faith necessary to bring it together. Those people were Kidder Meade for CBS, Richard Salant for NBC, and Alfred Schneider for ABC. Betsy Pleasants, chief financial officer for the Institute of Politics, is a master facilitator and supreme administrator who covered all my weaknesses and guaranteed that the potentially fatal slips between cup and lip did not occur.

Finally, a special word must be said about Jonathan Moore, director of the Institute of Politics, friend, colleague, and mentor for over twenty years, whose vision, persistence, competence, and commitment are contagious. Without his leadership, prodding, and advice, there would have been no conference and no book. If there are deficiencies in the product, I am largely responsible for them. If there are contributions, Jonathan Moore deserves much of the credit for them.

Photo by Martha Stewart

Moderator Floyd Abrams leading a discussion among the participants on Saturday afternoon in the ARCO Forum at the John F. Kennedy School of Government.

1

Introduction and Overview

Planning and Preparation

In the spring of 1981, CBS approached the Institute of Politics at Harvard's John F. Kennedy School of Government with a proposal. They suggested that the institute convene a group of academic experts to meet with senior CBS personnel to think through current laws and regulations that affect network coverage of the presidential election process.

The institute's response was that there was great interest in the subject matter but that both CBS and the institute ought to involve other institutions and individuals from the worlds of television and politics in such a gathering. Specifically, the institute recommended that such a proposal would be particularly exciting and potentially enormously productive if it came from all three major commercial networks.

CBS agreed to take the initiative and indicated a willingness to underwrite a third of the costs of the program if the other networks would do the same. Jonathan Moore, director of the Institute of Politics, approached ABC and NBC and, with a remarkable spirit of cooperation that confirmed the importance of the subject matter, all three networks signed on. In mid-August, representatives of the institute met with senior news and corporate executives from the networks to begin the planning process.

At that meeting, the agenda of the conference was expanded to include not only laws and regulations but also network policies and practices on election coverage and the conduct and performance of both the television personnel and the politicians involved in the presidential election process.

Content often follows form. Decisions agreed on about how many people would participate, how many participants would be invited from television, politics, and academia, and how the conference sessions would be structured all affected the nature of the dialogue (and therefore the subjects covered in this book). The planners' intention was that both sides of the media-politics connection would be examined. However, although both sides were examined, the conference became primarily centered on the networks' problems and performance in covering presidential elections, and the politicians got off too lightly.

Each network had five of the thirty-eight participants. There were also representatives from the BBC, Cable News Network, and Public Broadcasting Service. Retired senior network leaders Frank Stanton and Richard

Salant were official observers whose views were solicited at several points. The participants sat around a single table, each session had a general focus. Moderators asked questions and ordered the conversation, keeping it moving so that the agenda would be completed.

All the issues about coverage were raised, but, especially for the network participants, these problems and most of the suggested solutions had been raised before. What was new was the sense of sharing, and airing, those concerns. No one could remember when the networks had participated with each other in an open forum over an extended period of time, subjecting themselves to examination not only by politicians and academicians but by colleagues as well. The most telling moments of the weekend came when respected network correspondents and managers expressed doubts and worries usually heard only from outsiders. The most intense second-guessing came from the network participants themselves, often from the very people who had made the decisions and policies being discussed.

The problems explored that weekend are timely and essential for anyone concerned about the openness, effectiveness, and fairness of the presidential selection process; they go directly to the capacity of the voters to make intelligent, informed judgments about who is best to lead the country.

The conference did not deal with the current structure of the television industry nor with the presidential selection process itself. The focus instead was on the day-to-day questions confronting the networks and the politicians in their relations with one another. Underlying the entire discussion was the sense that even considering the constraints over which they had no control, both the networks and the politicians could do better at making the presidential election a full and robust public debate.

The Issues

The dialogue during that weekend did touch all the issues pertinent to the networks' influence on presidential elections.

Chapter 2 covers William Ward's opening address and the dialogue that followed it. The basic question that he posed was whether there are constraints inherent in the technology of television itself and in the way the industry is organized in this country that limit what the networks can do—and therefore can be held responsible for—in the presidential election process. In response, the network participants said that the constraints were not the main issue but rather what could be done to improve coverage of the next election season.

In chapter 3, which covers the first working session of the conference, Moderator Benno Schmidt, Jr., uses a hypothetical case to cover the entire landscape of presidential selection, from the early thoughts of potential candidates until election night itself. The most important questions considered in this session were:

What is the value of network coverage of the candidate—to the networks, the candidate, and the people—early in the campaign, in the year or so before the first of the caucuses and primaries?

Does the equal-time requirement unduly restrict network coverage of candidates and potential candidates as they are emerging?

How does a candidate get network coverage at various phases of the campaign?

What is the responsibility of the networks for allowing the candidate to present his or her views in an unfettered way at the announcement and at other important points in the process?

What factors govern how much time and money the candidates and the networks allocate to a particular primary or caucus?

Should the networks cover the conventions gavel to gavel?

Why are correspondents from the networks allowed on the convention floor, and what role do they play there?

What is the effect of exit polls and forecasting results on outcomes of other contests held on the same day?

In chapter 4, Moderator Floyd Abrams gave the network participants the opportunity to talk about their problems with the ways in which the networks and the candidates interact during the presidential campaigns. The central issues were:

To what extent do the networks try to determine which potential candidates to take most seriously?

Is the shrinking audience for network campaign coverage a result, or a cause, of declining interest in voting and in participating in the political process?

Are the networks constrained in their coverage by the need to appeal to the widest audience?

Why is so much of the coverage negative in tone?

Does the cynicism and manipulativeness of the candidates and their managers affect network correspondents' coverage of the campaigns?

Do thirty-second political commercials cheapen the electoral process?

Do the network correspondents communicate to the viewers in a short-hand that can be deciphered in all its nuances only by fellow insiders in journalism and the campaigns?

Is there too much coverage of personalities and the horse race and not enough coverage of issues?

Is the structure of the campaign calendar responsible for the difficulties of providing adequate coverage of the campaign?

Aren't the American people far better informed about their candidates than they have been in the past?

The session moderated by Anthony Lewis, covered here in chapter 5, was designed to probe the problems faced by the politicians and political strategists in dealing with the networks. Several questions provided the focus for the discussion:

How do the campaign managers try to control the messages about their candidates that are transmitted by the media?

What are the dangers inherent in live coverage of a breaking political story, and what can be done to minimize them?

Should the networks take the responsibility for criticizing the incumbent president if the opposition party is failing to do so effectively?

Are the networks too often making or reporting on their own news, as in, for instance, commissioning their own delegate and public-opinion polls?

Should the networks take into consideration, in their coverage and resource-allocation decisions, the views of the lawmakers and politicians about the relative importance of various events and stages of the process?

If the networks devoted more time to issues, would they thereby have too great a role in setting the national political agenda?

Are stories on the nightly news simply too short to do justice to the issues in a presidential campaign?

The last discussion session, moderated by Tyrone Brown and presented here in chapter 6, focused on the regulatory issues. Among the questions raised and considered were:

Does the original rationale for regulation of the electronic media, namely, scarcity of the airwaves, still apply?

Why are the networks unwilling to sell sizable chunks of prime time to candidates?

If the politicians could buy time whenever they wanted, would wealthy candidates and campaigns have unfair advantage?

Would it be better if networks were judged on their record of providing "reasonable access" over the life of their licences rather than on a case-by-case basis?

Does the equal-time law provide necessary protection for non-front runners and minor-party candidates, or does it unduly limit the opportunities for the networks to present the leading candidates to the people?

Would it be in the public interest to repeal the equal-time law for presidential candidates, allowing the networks to sponsor and arrange debates, but keep the law for other races in which local situations and issues create more possibilities for unfair coverage?

Do the candidates now have too much control over the terms and conditions of the debates?

Chapter 7 covers the final wrap-up session on the conference. Ithiel deSola Pool, who had been invited to attend the entire gathering and to present some reflections at the conclusion, made the initial remarks. His thoughts and those of the others who spoke at that final discussion are presented in edited form in the order in which they were delivered. Without further comment, they provide an appropriate conclusion to this book.

Emerging Attitudes

The chronology of the conference provides the organizing vehicle for this book, but the understanding of the relationships among the networks, the politicians, and the presidential election process go beyond the recitation and analysis of the specific issues discussed. Four themes seemed to emerge from the conference dialogue, taken as a whole.

Profits, Votes, and the Public Interest

If any single idea pervaded the conference, it was whether the short-term interests of the politicians in getting elected and those of the networks in getting viewers were in conflict with the public interest in a full and frank discussion of issues and the most thorough exposure to the candidates during the campaign. The professionals sitting around that table were the leaders in their business. They respected each other's goals and did not look on them cynically. Providing information to the public was a means as well as an end of their efforts. They unabashedly discussed policies and practices that sometimes undermine the kind of election process everyone desires. Richard Wirthlin, for example, analyzed the strategy of keeping the candidates away from the media. And Frank Reynolds explained and defended the "sour and sardonic attitude" that reporters conveyed to their audience.

In the intense daily competition for audience and votes faced by the networks and the politicians, how is the public's interest represented? Candidates are not going to accept debate conditions that they feel put them at a disadvantage. Networks are going to follow each other to overcover a meaningless caucus or straw vote.

Much of the squabbling at the conference took place over this kind of expediency; on an issue-by-issue basis, it often appeared that higher purposes were receiving short shrift on both sides. But coverage undoubtedly has improved considerably over the years, and the public is getting much more than it used to from television. The competitive pressures and the recent emergence of television news as highly profitable programming have had some positive consequences as well as negative ones. Yet within the networks themselves there are those who want to contribute more to the presidential selection process and those concerned with other program interests, broader business matters, and even other news stories clamoring for limited space.

An Adversarial Relationship?

Much has been written about the adversarial attitudes between the press and the politicians. There was every reason to believe that this conference would evince that hostility on both sides. What appeared, however, was quite different. For all their quarrels, the politicians and the network people seemed to be more like colleagues and symbionts than opponents. Ronald Brown described the relationship as "family." The politicians and the networks need each other, use each other, and are obsessed by each other's businesses. The politicians are media junkies and the network journalists are political junkies. They talk in codes that only fellow insiders—other politicians and their staffs, consultants, and other political reporters—can fully decipher.

The politicians and the journalists who cover them share an environment from which viewers and voters are excluded. The disagreements between the network people and the political people were differences in perspective and in interests but always seemed to be differences among players who were working the same side of the street. Each side had its goals, its pride, and its professionalism, as well as self-righteousness and defensiveness about its role in the process. There were, for example, two very different views of the ideal campaign. For the networks, it would be an election season in which there were no federal regulations, more time allotted for coverage, network participation in sponsoring regular debates, control over the selling of time to candidates, license for reporters to tell why things are happening as well as what is happening, plus responsibility for setting the issue agenda, particularly where the politicians were unwilling to do so. For the politicians, it would be a world with regulation to ensure fairness and equal time, with network news accepting the responsibility to serve as conduits for the candidates' messages, with access to paid time on their own terms, and coverage limited to their agendas rather than agendas initiated by the press or other interests.

The conference participants were men and women who had survived and prospered under the current system. Both the politicians and the network people had ideas for change, but the strong sense is that their recommendations, however lofty or rhetorical, were designed to increase their hegemony over the process. The corollary was that any change that did not work toward that end was worse, whatever its value to the public, than no change at all.

Tinkering with Form and Content

Throughout the conference, specific proposals were made to change the form and content of network campaign coverage in ways that might improve the dialogue during the presidential elections. In general, these suggestions were met with one of two responses: Either the network participants explained the problem as a function of the complexity of the pressures on network television, or they pointed to the way the politicians conducted the campaigns as forcing them into certain decisions about coverage.

Presidential campaigns are not run for the primary purpose of enlightening the voters and engaging in full debate; the goal is to win. The public must rely on the other contenders—and the media—to hold a candidate accountable for his warts as well as his beauty marks. That does not relieve the networks of their responsibility to the process; it intensifies it. It also suggests that a dialogue strictly between the networks and the politicians will not likely produce better information for the voters in the next campaign. Academicians, other experts, and interested citizens must also be involved in the debate.

Regulatory Issues: The Power of Decision

A less than charitable observer would view the debate over the regulatory issues as matters of power and self-interest. To be sure, Congress does not often pass legislation that would hinder politicians in general or incumbents in particular in their campaign tactics. For their part, networks are usually found making principled arguments for a position on a regulatory question that happily coincides with their business and journalistic self-interest as well. But the regulatory issues, particularly the two emphasized at this conference, do come down to matters of who should decide.

For reasonable access [Section 312 (a) (7) of the Communications Act (1934)], the issue at the conference was who should decide when the campaign is to begin for the purpose of requiring the networks to provide access for candidates, in particular, requiring them to sell time.

The discussion of the equal-opportunity law [Section 315 (a) of the Communications Act (1934), usually referred to as "equal time"] and the matter of debates went along similar lines. The networks said that the politicians have too much control now over the organization of debates; and the politicians said that if the networks could run debates and decide who participates, they would have too much power and could shut out non-front runners in the early stages of a presidential campaign.

This society has allowed these issues to be sorted out and resolved by the courts and the regulatory agencies, as if those forums seemed likely to produce more flexible and fair resolutions than if either the politicians or the networks were left alone to make the decisions.

Be that as it may, the willingness of these senior network journalists to discuss issues so important to them and so central to their own professional success, in an open forum, together with colleagues and competitors from other networks and counterparts from the world of politics is an important statement in itself. It is testimony to their commitment to play a more constructive role in the electoral process. And it signifies an awareness of the power they do exercise. The result of their participation in the dialogue reported in this book is a unique view of the potential and limits of the force of network news on presidential politics.

2 Back to Basics

Major Dramatis Personae (in Order of Appearance)

John William Ward, President-Elect, American Council of Learned Societies

Tom Brokaw, News Correspondent, NBC News

Adam Clymer, Political Correspondent, *New York Times*

Jeffrey Gralnick, Vice-President and Executive Producer, Special Events, ABC News

Martin Plissner, Political Director, CBS News

George Reedy, Nieman Professor of Journalism, Marquette University

Ben H. Bagdikian, Professor, Graduate School of Journalism, University of California at Berkeley

Robert MacNeil, Executive Editor, "The MacNeil-Lehrer Report"

Richard Wald, Senior Vice-President, ABC News

David Webster, U.S. Director, British Broadcasting Corporation

John D. Deardourff, Chairman of the Board, Bailey, Deardourff and Associates

The opening session of the conference was designed to set the table for the rest of the weekend. Jonathan Moore, director of the Institute of Politics, noted that the purpose of the conference was most definitely not to tell anyone what to do about their problems but for all the professionals assembled in the room—journalists, politicians, and academics—to "find ways of evoking insights and guidance and ideas about our problems from others, in order to figure out the answers for ourselves. And even that kind of assistance," he continued, "just isn't going to be that clear and conclusive." William Ward, a historian and former president of Amherst College and now president of the American Council of Learned Societies, was asked to provide some historical perspective on the relationship between the media and presidential elections. He might have chosen an easy route by simply recounting stories of elections past. Instead, he set out on a more ambitious course, attempting to place the impact of the media on presidential elections in the broader context of changes in the relationships among institutions in society as a whole.

The implication of his message was that what the networks can and cannot do about the presidential elections is limited by factors and forces outside the control of those in the audience, both the politicians and the television professionals. But the message was received by the network representatives at the conference as a challenge to their professionalism. They responded with challenges of their own and with their defenses up.

Ward's Address

Ward began by pointing out that in the landmark work *Public Opinion*, Walter Lippmann explored the question of how Americans form their view of reality by using the techniques of a cultural anthropologist:

> Lippmann's way of looking at the public, at society, is to try to understand the way people behave, the way they think, the institutions in society as different forms of action which are particular expressions of a general pattern of meaning which defines the culture. . . .

Ward proposed to examine a moment of American history in the same way, exploring connections between media and the elections of that time, and then, by analogy, raising questions about that connection now. The moment he chose was the Jacksonian period, the era when the political party emerged as a legitimate political institution. Ward said that the experience was somewhat analogous to the present because then as now technological changes enabled the press to become "both the instrument of and the shaper of mass democratic politics."

Prior to Andrew Jackson, Ward continued, politics were élite: Candidates for president were picked by a small group of leaders. The notion of mass political parties was new. Jackson and his Democratic party rose on the wave of two major social changes: the expansion of the frontier and the Industrial Revolution, which dominated that period. Either of these movements would have caused new arrangements. Together they were "wrenching." In the business of elections, they worked together to destroy what Ward characterized as "the politics of deference to established élites." Jackson achieved power through "the emergence of the ordinary common man as a participant in politics." He talked in his inaugural address about public duties being so "plain and simple" that the average citizen could perform them. The parties emerged, and here Ward quoted Martin Van Buren, one of the great architects of American party politics, "to create new party feelings to keep those masses together."

Thus, Ward went on, the parties arose "to give shape to and voice to the will of the majority of people outside of government." The parties needed leaders, professional party politicians like Van Buren and others, to maintain them and give them coherence, continuity, and some element of discipline. Their medium for doing that, now made possible by new technology, was the newspaper, which for the first time could reach the public widely and cheaply. The newspapers of that day were organs of the political parties, at the same time coming out of and feeding the new social and political order.

What was the significance of this 1820s history lesson for a gathering of political and network people in the 1980s? Ward explained:

> Democratic politics did not create the mass newspaper, and the mass newspaper did not create democratic politics. It was not a case of cause and effect. Both of them were manifestations of historical change which required new values and new institutional forms. To put it another way, if one wishes to understand the relation between the media and the Presidential elections of Andrew Jackson and Martin Van Buren, one cannot do so simply by studying the effect of the media on Presidential elections. One must accept the necessity of trying to understand the general culture of that period in time.

In the same way that the development of the newspapers and mass politics can be understood in terms of broader societal changes and not in terms of cause and effect on each other, so in the present time, Ward argued, "television and contemporary politics may . . . be separate manifestations of changes which are greater than either of them and which shape them both."

If wrestling with whether television had created current politics or whether it is the other way around is addressing the wrong question, what, in Ward's view, were the questions that ought to be asked? Ward listed four:

> First, what are the values implicit in the technology of television as a mode of communication?

> Then, second, what are the values of television as an institution; that is, its ownership, its management, and the economic imperatives which drive it?

> Then I think we should ask, what are the values, and the institutional expression of them, which we think characterize, or should characterize, a decent democratic political process?

> Then, of course, we could ask whether the values of television, the values of television both technically and institutionally, are or are not compatible with the democratic political process.

Ward suggested four examples of values inherent in the technology of television: television generates passivity in its viewers, the sender of the message is in control; television simplifies the subjects it is communicating about; television conveys immediacy; and television generates emotional intensity. Then he discussed possible implications for the political process of those values of the medium.

For instance, Ward suggested that television's quality of passivity has led to an interest in interactive video communication. Through such involvement, some people think it might be possible to combat the sense of impotence that the viewer must feel from seeing so much on television that affects his life but that is completely out of his control. Ward suggested that rather than making the video experience interactive, a better political response to the passivity of television might be to look for ways to give the average person the means for more control over those aspects of his life that are closest to him: his work, his home, his community. Such involvement would be a counterforce to whatever alienation from society in general and the political process in particular is generated by television. Or, to take another example, one that goes to the heart of the role of television in the political process, Ward noted that television's pressure toward simplification makes it a difficult medium for conveying complexity and ambiguity. He quoted John Chancellor as saying that "politicians deal in a world of complexity, and television deals in a world of simplicity."

What follows, argued Ward, is that if "our sense of democratic politics requires that modern man have some tolerance for ambiguity, some understanding of the complexity of modern life, then television is not the medium by which to educate him to it." Do not ask or expect television, the message was, to do what it cannot do. Rely on television not to educate the electorate, which it cannot do, but to convey emotion and satisfy the need for immediacy by bringing events into homes as they are happening, almost as if the viewers were there.

Ward then looked at the institutional values of television. He noted that, unlike most other countries, the United States organized its television in private, profit-making corporations. Consequences flow from that fact: Profit comes through advertising, and under the present circumstances all three networks are therefore driven to seek the largest audience and thus to search for the common denominator in programming that will entertain the most people. The result of that imperative, he continued, is to create a bias against the "variety and multiplicity of American society" and a tendency toward entertainment that is positive and upbeat. All entertainment is not happy, but it is usually positive in the sense that it carries with it an implication that if there is a problem, there must be a solution as well.

Here, Ward argued, there is a serious implication for politicians. Television is not a good medium for those seeking or in public office who wish to educate the public about the intractability and complexity of some of the problems that confront "an advanced technical society in an international world where no nation has complete control over its destiny."

John William Ward, President-Elect, American Council of Learned Societies; and Tom Brokaw, News Correspondent, NBC News.

Photo by Martha Stewart

An Aggressive Response

Tom Brokaw was the first to respond to Ward's request for questions. He asked Ward, "How much television do you watch?" Ward answered "very little," and when that provoked some murmuring in the audience, Ward asked Brokaw why he was interested in the answer. Brokaw said that he wanted to know because Ward had "come to some fairly strong conclusions about what it is that we do and the reaction that we engender in who it is that watches us. . . ." Brokaw suggested that Ward's views might have been based on "some personal experiences" in addition to "incomplete research."

Ward answered Brokaw's challenge with three separate points. First, he recounted his experience with television news during the period when he served as chairman of a commission investigating corruption in Massachusetts government. At one point his commission held fourteen weeks of public hearings, and the story was on the front pages of the newspapers and on the local nightly news almost every day. It was the one time in his life when he watched television news every night, and he came to some conclusions based on that experience about what television does to news:

> You had three minutes on an oil spill in Somerville, three minutes on the Arab-Israeli peace talks, three minutes of the commission. . . .
>
> When that happens, two things: the world becomes homogenized, that is, the same voice is telling you about all these things, and so things have a sort of equal weight. . . .
>
> Secondly, you may have a sense that you know something is going on, but you don't know anything about it and you walk away with the illusion that you are informed. . . .

Second, Ward tried to restate his thesis in a way that would be more sympathetically received by the network people in the audience: "I tried to use a historical analogy to suggest that television has been blamed for more than it deserves to get blamed for."

Neither tack had done much to calm the expressions of indignation in the audience, and Ward was becoming exasperated and a bit more strident himself:

> I really was trying to say to you that I think television is getting blamed for things which are a function of the conditions of modern society, and that to ask the question of the relations between the media and elections as separate things is probably naive. . . . You cannot understand what you are doing, and you cannot understand what the politicians are doing unless you understand the other social and economic forces which are creating the conditions of contemporary American society. You are probably miss-

ing what the hell is going on by being either so self-defensive or self-important. . . .

Ward's three responses were interlaced with comments from participants, which aggressively challenged him for what they perceived to be his criticism of them and their work. For the most part, during this part of the discussion, the print journalists joined with their electronic brethren. Here are a few of those remarks:

> Brokaw: You are judging us as a kind of mono voice, and that mono voice is drawn from your experience on those three minutes in the local news . . . when we don't pretend to be the only voice within the electronic medium, and certainly within the wider spectrum that is represented by all of the media. . . .

> Adam Clymer: You gave a long list of what television does in covering elections. I think that any of the people whom I know from the television industry have more serious questions about the problems of trying to do what they are trying to do, which is generally serious, and as serious as what newspapers are trying to do or as serious as what professors are trying to do, than you seem to have given them credit for.

> Jeffrey Gralnick: You began by saying, "I'm not sure if I know what I'm talking about; however, here is an indictment of what you do." I have only one question: What makes you think you are correct?

> We know what we are doing; we know what we are doing as professionals. We function as professionals day in and day out, . . . but you have fairly well indicted both the news business and the television news business, and why do you think you are correct?

> Martin Plissner: After having described what a great job of projecting emotion television does, you then describe pictures as great, too. But comment and anything involving intelligence is something that you don't expect in television. The condescension of the whole speech is not only that you didn't want to hear any more words, you just want to see the pictures.

> George Reedy: What came out to me and I think everybody else in the room is, what the devil are we going to do with television? You know it is here, it has changed things. How are we going to handle it?

> The simple answer to that is that we are going to adjust to it, just as we have always adjusted to everything in our history. I don't think the voters are dumb. I think that when a new method of communication comes along, the voters adjust to it; and I think the politicians adjust to it. And sooner or later it becomes a normal part of the way the nation handles its politics. . . .

> The facts of life are that we're going to live with it; television is going to do what it has to do, simply the way the old media did what they had to do. And if we could do something here, it is to give some understanding as to what these things are that we have to do.

In the middle of this part of the discussion, Christopher Arterton had tried to bring the conversation back to a less volatile level by asking the journalists to be precise about what they, as professionals, heard in Ward's remarks that they found objectionable. But it was not until Reedy's comments, and Ben Bagdikian's response to them, that the dialogue began to shed as much light as heat on the issues Ward had tried to address.

A More Constructive Dialogue

Bagdikian asked Reedy why the gathering was taking place if television were so immutable. Ward asked him whether his notion that people would adapt to the role of television meant a kind of technological determinism wherein people cannot really decide for what purposes they will make use of the technology. Reedy answered that he was really saying that people would learn to understand television and to use it and control it "in their own particular way."

Lewis Wolfson picked up on this point and argued, "To say that we're creatures of our society and the forces around us seems to be an easy historian's view." He suggested that everyone at the conference wanted to focus on some of "the incremental things that can be done" to improve television's coverage of presidential elections; and he called on the journalists, as Arterton had before him, to focus on specific concerns.

Brokaw then delivered another response to Ward's speech, this one much less hostile and instinctive. His remarks created the tone for the rest of the evening discussion and, in particular, set the stage for monologues by Robert MacNeil, Richard Wald, and David Webster, which acknowledged the validity of the basic assumption behind Ward's address and began to build on it in preparation for the discussion of the details of the relationship between the politicians and the networks to take place over the next two days.

Brokaw said that, as a television person,

> my argument is that your premise is primitive, that there are problems in television that I came here to spend the next three days addressing, because I know them, I think, quite well, and I'm concerned about them. . . .
>
> I think you are starting at an elementary level. While I would concede that many of your conclusions are correct, we have different, larger, more sophisticated kinds of problems that we all ought to be dealing with here.

MacNeil argued with Brokaw's assessment of Ward's premise, but in doing so, advanced the discussion substantially. Ward's point, he said, is

> very simple, but very profound. . . . It is an attempt to address those values which may be inherent in the technology itself and those that may be

imposed on the technology, and the way it is used, by the values of those institutions that use it. I think that is central to all of this, and the other problems all flow from it. . . . And central to that is the commercial value and the need to maximize the audience. . . . It is very simple, but it is absolutely right, and everything flows from that.

Wald followed MacNeil and picked up on the idea that there was much to commend in what Ward had to say. He then took the conversation further in explaining the nature of the television journalists' concerns and their hopes for the gathering:

To all of our regret, Dick Salant once upon a time said that the news in a television report would only fill up five columns of the *New York Times*. He neglected to add that there were pictures too. The pictures convey a form of information that we are finding it difficult in our own lexicon to describe. Their complexity, the manipulation of those realities, which in books is done from prejudices not explained, is done in pictures from prejudices half visible, but for which there are still no words.

We are now at the edges of ways of dealing in terms of how to describe those pictures, and how to describe that complexity of effort that is not yet clear or clean. If we are lucky, we will find for ourselves a few words this weekend and maybe some other ways of describing what we so. But to approach it as though it were . . . a simple process, is to approach it in a way that defeats analysis.

The troubles of television, in its dealings both with other pieces of the press and with our society, are troubles that no one has been able to disentangle; and the simplistic approach that says "it simplifies" does not help at all. It is a little bit insulting to come at this from the point of view that the thing that is most complex for us is to you the simplest, when you don't seem to have the tools to discuss the problems we see. . . .

I would willingly hear you all over again, and would try not to be visceral in my reaction, if I felt that you would look at us with the same amount of complication with which we are already looking at ourselves. . . .

We are professional and we want you to tell us something because we find lacking in our professional discussion such tools as academia normally brings to us, that would help us enlighten the problems of which we are presently aware, but cannot, for the future, see a solution.

As Wald concluded, John Deardourff commented that he

could not help but remember both that it was his [Wald's] network that refused to televise live the first television debate of 1980 and then charged 50 cents a call to solicit views of voters about the results of the second debate. I hope we will get to those questions before the weekend is over.

Finally, in what became the last monologue of the evening, Webster brought the discussion full circle, incorporating the thrust of Ward's discourse with the more constructive elements of the criticism that followed it:

One of the fascinating and delightful things about a profession which actually believes in what it is doing is that, quite naturally, when attacked, they are defensive. People who have a more cynical relationship to their profession regard it purely as a matter of dollars and cents.

Television is a medium which happens to be better as a medium of experience, than as a medium of exposition. It is not actually very good at explaining things. . . . It is also a medium of homogenization of attitudes. Also, we have real problems about attention span, and what we are doing to people's ability to concentrate on subjects for more than two and a half minutes—which is built in structurally—the resolution of problems. Somehow, once a problem has been dealt with on television, you may feel that it has been done, dealt with in real life.

There is also a problem of polarization of attitudes, and I think one of the things which is most worrying is something you just touched on, the difficulty of dealing with ambiguity.

This is not to be defensive about the medium. . . . But there are real problems. You have pointed to some of them, and quite properly some of the people in the profession have responded saying it is not quite like that. And this, I think, is a reasonable healthy dialogue.

Afterword

A healthy dialogue? Yes, perhaps, but an awkward one as well. At the low point of the conversation, Brokaw was referring to the non-television people in the room as adversaries. At its most lucid, Wald was acknowledging the truth in what Ward had to say but pleading for the participants in the conference to get beyond it and wrestle with the problems of dealing with presidential elections as the television professionals see them. Ward's message, that television was being blamed for problems that were well outside its capacities, should have given more comfort than it did to those in both television and politics who were more focused on finding incremental changes for doing it better the next time around and on defending past performances. And his reiteration of the limitations of the medium imposed both by the technology and by the institutional organization of the industry only served to remind the television professionals of the baggage they bear and the hurdles they need to overcome in order to do the job which the best of them very much want to do. By raising questions on a fundamental level about the capacity of television to contribute to the election process in a way that furthers the democratic dialogue, Ward temporarily opened horizons to larger issues. That Ward was asking good questions would be well borne out by the recurrence of his themes throughout the conference. It was evident, however, that he had raised them in such a way as to provoke an initial reaction by some of the network participants of defensiveness and counter-criticism. It was clear that the challenge of the conference was at least as difficult as anticipated and that real reflection and self-scrutiny would take more time, trust and commitment, and engagement on specific issues during the weekend.

3 Friendly Foes Focus on a Hypothetical Presidential Campaign

Major Dramatis Personae (in Order of Appearance)

Benno C. Schmidt, Jr., Moderator, Professor of Law, Columbia Law School

Richard B. Wirthlin, President, Decision/Making/Information

David R. Gergen, Assistant to the President for Communications, The White House

David L. Garth, President, Garth Group

Gerald Rafshoon, President, Rafshoon Communications

John D. Deardourff, Chairman of the Board, Bailey, Deardourff and Associates

Adam Clymer, Political Correspondent, *New York Times*

William Small, President, NBC News

William Leonard, President, CBS News

Tom Brokaw, News Correspondent, NBC News

Jeffrey Gralnick, Vice-President and Executive Producer, Special Events, ABC News

Frank Reynolds, Chief Anchor, World News Tonight, ABC News

Richard Wald, Senior Vice-President, ABC News

Henry Geller, Director, Washington Center for Public Policy Research

Edwin Diamond, Editorial Director, *Ad Week*

The first working session of the conference used a hypothetical case as a vehicle for getting the issues out on the table. The notion was to follow a campaign chronologically, stopping at each turning point to raise the questions about the relationship between the networks and the politicians that would be probed and analyzed in the subsequent sessions. Inevitably, the conversation went deeply into a few subjects as well as generating the broad agenda. By the end of the morning, the ground had been covered. Every aspect of a campaign was touched, from the early musings of an ambitious U.S. senator, wondering whether this will be his shot at the brass ring, to election night itself.

The Early Stages

Moderator Benno Schmidt began by asking Congressman David R. Obey to assume the role of a U.S. senator, thinking about running for president about three years before the election. Congressman Obey said that even at that stage television would play an important role. One test of viability of the candidacy would be whether money could be raised, and "that's determined pretty much by whether you can show up in the polls at all. And that in turn is determined in large part by whether you can get any visibility at all in television."

Schmidt advanced the case: Assuming the senator is already pretty well known and shows up in the polls, how is the decision made whether or not to run? Who would be consulted? Richard Wirthlin identified five questions to be considered:

> One, where do I stand with the public at large? What are my natural constituencies? What kind of issues have I been dealing with; are they issues that are likely to carry me through the initial and secondary stages of the campaign?
>
> Second, I would want to do a very careful assessment of my supporting party, touch base with those who play a national role as far as the party is concerned, but perhaps even more importantly than that, assess what kind of party support I have in some of the critical primary states.
>
> And thirdly, I would want to know, as precisely as I could, what the assets and political liabilities were of my opponents.
>
> Fourth, what kind of personal support could I get from those who have gone through Presidential campaigns in the past?
>
> Fifth, what kind of access might we have to the media?

David Gergen suggested that access to the national media is helpful but not crucial at the early stage. He said that if he were going off to a cabin to decide whether to run, he would take with him an organizer, a finance person, a media and polling person, a personal counselor ("a wise man type"), and his wife. Rather than media exposure, Gergen added, what a candidate needed most at this point was "a good network of people . . . and the making of a national organization." For Gergen, those are the elements necessary to do well in the early primaries and caucuses, and doing well in those events will bring the necessary national media exposure.

Schmidt asked how the connection between a media/polling person and the candidate is made. David Garth suggested that one factor for the consultant would be whether the people in the media think the candidate can "cope with the issues." Gerald Rafshoon added that a candidate would be likely to rely in the early decision making on a consultant with whom he had been associated before, in his senate campaign, for instance. At that point it is more important, he felt, to involve people who are close to him than those with national professional reputations. John Deardourff offered his views:

> You begin with the proposition that almost everybody who runs for president loses, so you try to decide which of this field of people . . . seem to have some reasonable prospect. And that question involves, I think, potential to raise money. . . . That is one measure of a credible candidate. A second measure of the credible candidate is the extent to which you would expect that candidate to be taken seriously.
>
> Then I would want to be . . . comfortable with that candidate's position on whatever range of issues are going to have to be the guts of their rationale for running. But aside from that personal consideration, I think you have to convince yourself that a candidate is in fact capable of presenting himself or herself and that issue mix, whatever it is, effectively.
>
> Then you do get into that question, is this a candidate who has some prospect of making that kind of effective presentation to a mass national audience?

The candidate has decided to run. What kind of coverage does he seek between then and his announcement? Rafshoon said that it might be desirable to go without much coverage for a period of time:

> I think we've seen in recent years that campaigns that start early or candidates who are mentioned early and are followed around and are analyzed and dissected, tend to fall apart. I want a period for the candidate to make mistakes without having the glare of the national media.

Adam Clymer suggested that "the more I know they don't want me to write about it, the more I am interested." He noted that there is probably some difference between the candidate and his advisor on this point. The advisor, he said, is "perfectly right" not to want extensive media attention early on, but "the candidates much more than their advisors want that reinforcement of being taken seriously and having a television crew or a newspaper reporter from some national outfit along. It means something to the candidate even if the advisors don't think it is such a hot idea."

William Small added later in the discussion that one of the purposes a candidate might have for early television exposure is to make an impression on the consultants whom he is later going to ask to take him on.

William Leonard added that in the early going, the networks would probably not be interested in devoting much time to a potential candidate who was not very well known. There was a strong sense that the best publicity for the candidate at this point would be related to issues with which he is associated in his official capacities. If he takes a leadership role on those issues, as Harold Bruno said, "the media will take care of itself in the normal course of events."

Garth emphasized the point by mentioning the danger of a candidate's getting involved in a wide-ranging interview before he was ready for it: "If he has an issue that he can stick to on the nightly news, that's fine." Garth indicated that a candidate cannot manufacture a position on an issue at this stage of running for president; he needs to get coverage with issues with which he is already identified. Garth suggested ways in which the candidate could increase coverage with such an issue:

> It could be the kind of issue that would lead you to speak to groups or rallies in various cities. You can do it with hearings in Washington, you can do it with investigations, you can do it with making reports available to the press.

Tom Brokaw pointed out that too often people thinking of candidate coverage consider only the nightly news and forget the opportunities presented by the morning programs and the weekend programs. The morning shows, he said, can be a kind of "out of town tryout" because the appearance can be confined to a specific issue before a limited audience. The nightly news, he added, is "a harder thing to crack at this stage; they are less interested in it, and we're less interested in it." Deardourff talked about the nightly news as being high-quality exposure for the candidate, but getting on is not an easy thing to do:

> You have got to work very hard, and you never know whether that work is going to produce anything. You can send this guy to California to speak to a rally of 5,000 people, but if the news judgment in New York is that something else that day is significantly more important, you have wasted a lot of time and money, and achieved nothing.

Even if he does make the nightly news, Garth and Brokaw pointed out, coverage would amount to only a line or two. Brokaw added that even if Deardourff's trip to California did not produce coverage on the nightly news, it would likely generate substantial time on the local news, which has huge viewership and great impact in the area in which it is seen.

Rafshoon reemphasized his point about the risks of early exposure on television:

> We are dealing with a medium that constantly bangs away at whatever this person is up to. And I don't think I would want this candidate getting that much national exposure this early. He is going to want it, but there are so

many other things he needs to do. I would rather have him in Iowa organizing. I would rather have him in New Hampshire making some friends. . . . I'd rather have him raising some money and preparing to be the candidate that he is going to be next year. Whether it is an issue, or positioning him in the consciousness of the people, you don't go out and put your road show on Broadway until you have played it out on the road.

Should a candidate in this position agree to do a long, in-depth interview, such as the one Senator Edward Kennedy did with Roger Mudd before he announced his candidacy in 1979? Ronald Brown said that the decision would depend on who the candidate is:

If he is not well known nationally, does not have much national exposure, hasn't had and doesn't have much recognition, you might want to test some things out.

Bruce Morton agreed. The best exposure at this stage would be around the issue or issues on which the candidate was basing his campaign.

The Announcement

The announcement is a television event. David Garth:

I think in this day and age, any announcement has to be planned with television in mind, primarily because the way it operates is the print press follows the television cameras, and you get your largest exposure on TV. So you are looking for a location or a setup to be apropos.

Sometimes if it is a senator, you want to have it in the Senate, because it works, it's in Washington. Sometimes you want to pull away and not to identify with Washington, and you have the announcement outside of Washington, to emphasize the new federalism. . . .

You want to see who else is in the field. If there is a very strong front-runner, you may want to let that person burn out for a while. You may want to delay your start, if in fact your candidate has some identification. If he has no identification, you want to get him out as early as possible, and maybe you want to get him out away from Washington. The physical location of where you do it would obviously be with television in mind. . . . I think what you want to do is to have as apropos a visual impact as possible.

What is the impact of the equal-time requirement on the timing of the announcement? Once a candidate announces, in many instances a station would be obliged to offer all announced candidates equal time once one announced candidate appears. The announcement itself is a bona fide news event and could be shown on the nightly news without triggering equal time. But because of equal time, according to Garth, "You do your opening, and then you disappear for two months." Ideally, he added, the candidate could choreograph the process: "first local talk shows, then move up to the network talk shows and the PBS talk shows and things like that, and then go to your announcement." This serves the dual purpose of generating exposure before the equal-time requirement is in effect and giving the candidate some "training" opportunities before he is a formal candidate.

Bruno noted that the announcement is "nothing more than a ceremony" since everyone knows by then that the candidate is a candidate. Why, asked Schmidt, do the networks put the announcement on the nightly news? Bruno defended the practice by saying that the fact that the candidate has made the formal decision to run is news, and besides, it does not get very much time on the air.

Clymer added that ceremonial or not, the announcement was

> an important moment for a candidate. It is the one time, until after he has won something, when he can almost certainly count on getting on television with what he wants to say about his candidacy; not very long, but it is one shot at saying "This is what I care about. This is why I think I ought to be your president." . . .
>
> From then on, when he gets on television and when he gets into the newspapers is very chancy.

Does the candidate really get his full message on the air at the time of the announcement? Small said that the amount of time he gets, whether or not it will be more than fifteen seconds, will be determined by how well known he is and by whatever else is happening in the world that evening. How then does the candidate make sure that the right message, the best fifteen seconds, is the one that makes the news?

Rafshoon said that if the candidate attacked the incumbent president, that would get coverage. But if you "talk about what your issues are," he wondered whether that would be used. Jeffrey Gralnick suggested that focusing on the actual words that made the air was missing the point. It is not just the amount of air time or which words of the candidate are used, but

> what else surrounds the piece of the candidate saying his or her best shot. If the correspondent and the producers involved have done their homework, that piece of sound with the candidate will be surrounded with a lot of factual information.
>
> Does the candidate have a Garth or a Rafshoon? Does the candidate have any organizational strength? Where does the candidate stand in the polls?
>
> This will be a fully framed political report that could possibly devastate this

candidate by indicating that, while an announcement was being made, there was no real political strength surrounding the performance.

Rafshoon jumped in here; Gralnick had identified an issue on which the interests of the candidate and the network were very different indeed. Both sides claimed to be representing the people and the public interest. Rafshoon asked rhetorically whether Gralnick's "factual information" was "what the public wants to know about a candidate when he announces? . . . Don't you think the public ought to have a chance to know what his issues are and what he stands for?" Gralnick defended the practice:

> The public should have an opportunity to know it all, and you, on your first day unveiling a candidate, want only issues. I would like some other facts thrown into the mix, just so there is more of an understanding of the reality of this very early announcing candidate.

Judy Woodruff reinforced Gralnick's view, suggesting that about a third of the typical one-minute-thirty- or one-minute-forty-second announcement piece would be the candidate's own words, probably the strongest words he used, and the rest "setting up who he is."

Schmidt wondered whether the candidate or his consultant could control or at least influence which words of the candidate would get on the air. Deardourff explained:

> You craft that statement in a way that any one of four or five or six paragraphs would be satisfactory to you if those were the ones that were selected.

Deardourff continued, sharpening the differences between the networks and the politicians on this point and emphasizing the impact that the media have on the candidate's strategic thinking:

> I think that the more interesting observation, and the one that would in many times control the timing of the announcement, is exactly the kind of realization that what you are likely to get is a very short piece on what the candidate said and a much longer piece on the double-think of why he said it and where he said it and that kind of analysis, or whatever you want to call it.
>
> This is the constant tension . . . between our interest in having people hear what the candidate has to say and the news media's interest in telling us more about why he or she is saying it at that particular time and place.
>
> There is one other thing that keeps running through my mind. . . . There is some mystique about the announcement date for a candidate which virtually guarantees coverage. . . . So the staging of the announcement becomes

important, and there is a process of negotiation, which obviously the general public is not aware of, that goes on between the campaign and the media.

Deardourff described that negotiation as "discussions over a period of days about what can we expect" if the announcement is made in one location or another. The conversations are held with the assignment desks of the news outlets:

> You describe to them what you are thinking of doing, and they then tell you whether they think that is something that mechanically, or from a news judgment, they are interested in covering. If they say "No soap," then you go back and retool your whole announcement.

Plissner, Clymer, and Leonard all objected to the characterization of the process as a negotiation, especially where the networks and presidential candidates are involved. Garth suggested that it is not exactly a negotiation, but "you want to make the coverage as convenient for them as possible."

Reedy suggested that all this strategic thinking on the part of the candidates, particularly insofar as it was discussed with the news organizations in advance, would naturally lead the media to emphasize the strategy, rather than the message. He recounted the story of a recent candidate for mayor in Milwaukee by way of illustrating his point:

> He made the announcement from his parents' house in South Milwaukee, because he wanted to identify with the proletarian Polish population of South Milwaukee.

> So what happened?

> Every television station that carried the announcement also pointed out that he lived in a very nice large house with a swimming pool on the North Side of Milwaukee, and for weeks the newspapers carried that story over and over again.

Elizabeth Drew closed the discussion of the campaign up to the announcement by warning against too mechanistic an approach to the process. The process of making a decision to run is made over an extended period, with many conversations. And while the announcement is surely important, she said, the candidacy is also substantially affected by what is written in the newspapers before and after that event and by word of mouth throughout the entire early period of the campaign.

Iowa: The First Test

What are the factors that govern how much time and money the candidates and the networks decide to allocate to a particular primary or caucus? The question elicted the first chicken-or-egg issue between the media people and the politicians. Here's how it went with reference to the Iowa caucuses:

> Wirthlin: Well, that would be a much easier decision to make, as to how much you should budget of time and money, if we knew how much the television was going to cover it.
>
> Schmidt: Is it the media focus that, more than anything else, makes you decide you had better hit Iowa, hit it hard?
>
> Wirthlin: Clearly it isn't the number of delegates. Clearly it is not the impact that Iowa may or may not have on the general election.
>
> Schmidt: Mr. Gralnick, why do you hit Iowa so hard?
>
> Gralnick: Because candidates hit Iowa so hard.

Congressman Obey said that in the 1980 campaign he urged Congressman Morris Udall, then a candidate for the Democratic nomination for president, to change plans and emphasize Iowa "because that was what the press was watching." The network people then began to defend their effort in Iowa on grounds other than the fact that the candidates were also making a great effort there.

Roger Mudd and Frank Reynolds argued that it was worthy of the attention simply because it was "the first test" for any of the candidates. Bruno noted that doing well in Iowa will attract national attention because it is first, but a good campaign there will have to concentrate on the local, not the national, media in order to succeed.

Still, it is a somewhat circular debate. Winning Iowa is important to the candidates primarily because the national media will make so much of the success; and the national media explain making such a fuss over Iowa and its victor because it is the first time the candidates have actually gone head to head against one another. But some candidates, such as President Reagan and Congressman Udall went to Iowa in 1980, so their managers said, primarily because they knew the media would give great emphasis to the results.

Richard Wald had a pendulum rather than a circle to explain the media presence. Iowa had been undercovered, in the media's view, in earlier presidential campaigns. Results were surprising. Candidates emerged. And the networks make sure that the next time they will not miss the Iowa story. When the candidates realize the media's coverage commitments, they rearrange their plans, which had been based on the undercoverage of the past. Wald suggested that if the results in Iowa are not conclusive, if "nobody comes up a winner, there is no clear consensus as to what happened . . . then four years later nobody will go to Iowa again."

Wald went on to say that in 1980 the networks changed their plans and increased their resources for Iowa when it appeared that there would be more candidates there than had been anticipated when the budgets were developed a year or more before. Brokaw pointed out that network re-source-allocation decisions depend not only on what the candidates are doing but also on what the other networks are doing. If one goes, the others will follow: "Maybe Cronkite is going to anchor from there, so we've got to get Chancellor there, and then Reynolds has got to go, and then the morning shows have to go."

Clymer noted that the newspapers too are part of the cycle of escalation of attention, and when that attention is given to Democratic contests in Iowa and New Hampshire there are particularly serious implications because those states are so very unrepresentative of the Democratic Party nationally. Neither, he pointed out, has a city with a population of over 200,000.

There was a strong feeling among the participants that wherever the first test took place, it would receive heavy national coverage. The politicians would spend a lot of time and money to do well because, particularly as long as it is in a small state and, like Iowa, a caucus state, it presents an opportunity to create momentum in a manageable environment.

Small made the last point on this matter and it contained another insight about the relationship between the networks and the politicians in the campaign:

> Everyone at this table says Iowa is exaggerated and not important and we shouldn't be there. We were all there. When we get to Iowa, everyone at this table is hungry to get into the game. The politicians are; the press is.

The Debates

Who gets invited to the debates? What is the format? How important is it that the networks cover the event live? And what conversations can and ought to take place between the debate sponsors and the networks about the arrangements?

Dot Ridings noted that the ideal is to include everyone who is an announced candidate, but in reality there has to be some judgment exercised, particularly in a very large field, about who ought to be included. Part of the reason why the number of candidates has to be limited is to make the event interesting enough to ensure that it will get network coverage.

It's a tricky situation. Under the 1975 ruling of the Federal Communications Commission, the networks could cover a debate live without triggering equal-time requirements for the candidates not participating if the debate was a "bona fide news event." A debate sponsored by the networks would not qualify because, as Leonard said, the networks would be organizing the event, not covering it. But if the goal, or one of the primary goals of the debate is to get live coverage in order to expose the candidates to more people, the networks' views on what would be worth covering are important. Yet, as Small pointed out, the networks could not even advise the sponsoring organization on whom should be invited or how it should be structured because "if you want to cover the debate, you cannot legally participate in the organization of it." Leonard said the networks "think the law is terrible," and Sharp agreed. Stephen Sharp added that even informal consultation with the debate sponsor, whether or not the network is actually helping, risks a charge that the network is colluding with the organizers and is no longer a disinterested observer of a bona fide news event.

Henry Geller, who initiated the action that resulted in the 1975 decision to interpret the equal-opportunities law to permit the networks to televise a debate that they had no hand in arranging, proposed a new expansion of that ruling: Allow the networks to arrange debates, on the theory that they were no less bona fide events just because the networks were involved. Ideally, Geller said, he would restrict the application of the equal-time provision only to paid time.

Geller was not concerned with the networks' excluding some candidates or handling the debate in a way that was perceived as favoring some over others. He recalled the experience in 1960 when Congress repealed the equal-time provisions, temporarily, and only for the presidential and vice-presidential candidates: "You got thirty-nine hours of coverage, you got the American people much better informed, and you didn't find any unfairness." The current law and interpretation, Geller continued, inhibits the networks from "being able to do whatever they want to do in trying to cover the campaign better." Congress has not repealed it, he added, because "they are all incumbents. They like equal time and want to keep it." Under probing from Schmidt as to why incumbents would favor a law that would seem to help less well-known candidates, Geller suggested that with the equal-time law there are fewer debates, and that's the way incumbents like it to be.

Sharp suggested that congressional opposition to repeal of equal time was not really well reasoned; if members of Congress

> sat down with their campaign advisors and looked at the totality of cam-
> paigning, the totality of these laws and their effect on the campaign, they
> would come to the conclusion that it is in their best interest to get rid of it.
> But what you are dealing with here is fifty years of habit and pattern and
> fear of the unknown.

Schmidt asked Sharp whether after the 1975 ruling, the law still really inhibited coverage of the campaign? Sharp thought it did affect the way the networks covered the campaigns, particularly with respect to special programs and documentaries. Leonard noted that the famous Mudd-Kennedy interview could not have been broadcast a few days later because Senator Kennedy announced his candidacy, and a broadcast following that would have triggered requests for equal time from, he recalled, thirteen or fourteen other candidates.

Paid Time

Schmidt asked Irwin Segelstein whether a candidate could buy five minutes of time for a noncontroversial, non-issue-oriented advertisement. Assuming the election process had begun, Segelstein said that the reasonable-access law and good journalistic judgment would suggest making the time available "subject to all of the give and take that occurs in these situations." Garth countered:

> It is very difficult to buy five minutes of any kind of decent prime time for an opening announcement or any kind of an announcement. The networks don't want to break into their regular programming. So they will give it to you at 5:45 or at 1:00 a.m.

Whether or not reasonable access was a good law would depend, Garth quipped, on whether his candidate was behind and needed to buy time or whether his client was ahead and less interested in getting on the air.

Rafshoon argued that the candidates "should have the option of starting their television campaign when they want to, just as the networks have the option of starting their coverage of the candidates when they want to." Wald commented that the networks deal in specific blocks of time, that five minutes is not one they ordinarily use, and that requiring them to sell that time would be like requiring a newspaper to print on slick paper when it never does so.

As to the content of the message, all seemed to agree that there was little control that the networks could or should exercise over the substance of what went on the air in paid time. As Segelstein said, the candidate "should have the right to present himself as he sees fit in his own commercials."

The Primaries

Schmidt asked Gergen whether he subscribed to the view that the networks put "too much emphasis on the horse race aspect of the primaries, who is ahead, what does the latest poll show, and that that emphasis comes at the expense of coverage of the substantive differences between the candidates on the issues."

Gergen responded that the studies he had seen indicated that television coverage is "about two-to-one in terms of time on horse race versus substance." Michael Robinson confirmed this view, citing his own study of the 1980 campaign. Further, Robinson said, if you compare horse race to coverage of policy issues ("substance" including more than just issues), the ratio on "CBS Evening News" during weekdays in the 1980 presidential campaign was about four to one. But Robinson then went on to point out that the important question is not the allocation of coverage but the impact of the coverage on the campaign and the electorate; on that score the picture was brighter. Robinson said there had been a dramatic increase in the last twenty years, since the age of campaign television, in the capacity of voters to identify where candidates stood on the issues. Since voters get most of their information about the campaigns from television, the networks must get some of the credit for the fact that the candidates' positions are getting through, despite the horse-race emphasis.

Schmidt asked Wirthlin whether the emphasis on the horse race by the media affects the conduct of the campaigns. Wirthlin said that there were some ways the campaign could influence how the networks cover the horse race, but they were limited:

> Select issues you know the press will cover with a higher degree of intensity. . . . But you raise an issue and the immediate question is, well, what happened inside the campaign, why was there a shift in emphasis, and you get right back into the politics and the discussion of the drama of the horse race.

Wirthlin added that campaigns look for the right visual environments for the candidate to feed the networks' emphasis on the horse-race aspects, but even though issues receive less coverage, they are the cutting edge of the campaign. Robinson agreed, citing the example of the announcement in 1980 that, if elected, Reagan would name a woman to the Supreme Court. Robinson suggested that the announcement was made knowing that it would be dissected politically by the media but also knowing, correctly, that the basic message would get through. They chose that issue at that time, Robinson said, because their polls showed them having problems getting support from women. Both messages got through, according to Robinson: the candidate's position and the media's explanation for why he was announcing it at that point in the campaign.

Wald found the discussion of this issue revealing; while the networks are citicized for too much emphasis on the horse-race aspects of the campaign, the politicians are determining and timing their issues based on horse-race considerations as well. "I find it embarrassing," he noted, "that the politicians think about their candidates the same way we do."

Robert MacNeil said that the horse race is what most people are interested in. Clymer added that it is really another chicken-or-egg question: The media are not covering the issues because the candidates are not talking about them. It was well into the campaign, March, according to Clymer, before George Bush made a substantive speech with an advance text and an opportunity for questions and analysis. And at that point, Clymer said, the only substantive speech Reagan had given was the statements about the North American Accord in his announcement.

Is the horse race the reality for both the media and the candidates, Schmidt asked? Brokaw made a telling point in response:

> The horse race changes all the time, and that's one of the reasons it gets attention. Whereas the positions on the issues don't change that much. They are not striking out every day with a new set of positions on the issues that are of greatest concern to us and the people they are trying to reach. They do that at the beginning. They have their positions that they strike, and we talk about them during the announcement. From then on it does become a horse race. . . . The change we are dealing with every day, what's new, what's different from yesterday, most often addresses itself to the business of the horse race.

Later in the discussion, Woodruff reemphasized Brokaw's view, suggesting not only that when the candidates say the same thing over and over again it is not news but also that the candidates really do not want the issues covered that thoroughly after they make their initial positions known.

Reynolds closed the discussion of horse race versus issue coverage by suggesting that the distinction is not all that clear between the two: The horse-race coverage provides documentation, analysis, and explanation for the movement in the campaign that rests very often on the candidates' positions on the issues.

The Convention

Schmidt turned the dialogue to coverage of the convention and began by asking Small how long in advance the networks make their plans. Small and Stuart Loory agreed that covering the convention was such a mammoth job that planning should begin two years ahead of time, long before it is clear who the candidates will be, never mind whether there will be a contest or a foregone conclusion. Schmidt followed that up by asking how the networks decide whether to cover it gavel to gavel.

Small suggested that the only news was who was on the ticket, but the convention did represent a unique opportunity to show the public "an entire political party, . . . the currents within that party and the issues that that party may or may not stand for." Small said that what the other networks were going to do would affect his decision, although he would not be influenced by knowing that one of the cable networks was going to provide full coverage.

Schmidt then raised the issue of whether the network correspondents ought to be allowed on the convention floor. Small acknowledged that it was "very strange that this is the one event where correspondents are indeed right among the players." But he argued for continuation of the practice:

> There are many things to be said, not just for the ease of coverage that we have, but for the opportunity to present the various currents within a political party by having us there.
>
> If we were not on the floor, I think it would be very difficult for the challenger to head off a movement for the front runner, and I think it is very important to have that opportunity.

Deardourff expressed concern at the implications of Small's rationale:

> If I thought Bill Small was right, that somehow having his correspondents on the floor was going to . . . materially alter the direction, then I think you could raise the question of whether they ought to be allowed to be there.
>
> It startles me, I must say, to hear him say that without his correspondents on the floor, you could not stop the front runner. It sounds as though he is suggesting that they are playing the game with us or something.

Small said that the network correspondents play an unusual communication role on the floor of the convention for the delegates themselves:

> It is a very strange phenomenon that people who are on the floor at the convention—I'm now talking about delegates—who do not have direct access to television (they don't have a set at their seats) seem to know instantaneously what is being said on television.

He suggested that candidates use the correspondents to communicate to the delegates:

> It's a lot quicker . . . to get a message out if correspondents are there. If we were banned from the floor of the convention, you the candidates would find us. If we were in the corridor, you would find us. If we were out in the parking lot, you would find us. It would just take a little longer.

Rafshoon agreed:

> Nobody wants to get the correspondents off the floor. You look for the correspondents.

Once again, it is not very clear who is using whom. At one point Small suggested that the correspondents influence the events, but by the end of the discussion everyone seemed to agree that the politicians used the network correspondents to carry messages to the delegates. Even though there is not a television set at every delegate's seat, it was accepted around the table that the delegates were somehow more aware of what was happening on television than what was happening on the podium.

Perhaps Brokaw best summed up the reasons why the convention is covered the way it is:

> I think it is entertaining, I think it is useful, and I think that even when the nominations are locked up it provides you with an opportunity to have a kind of dialogue about a lot of the issues that we have talked about here today. . . . It is just a combination of information and communication and time together and entertainment. As someone who cares about this subject of politics, it is a wonderful place to be, you know, wired to the world as it were.

Postconvention Coverage

Postconvention coverage is not complicated by the uncertainties and discretion that characterize the relationships between the networks and the candidates before the nominations. In opening this segment of the discussion, Rafshoon said that after the conventions, having the candidate on the nightly news too much was more of a worry than trying to get him on. He added that for a challenger, the schedule ideally is organized so that there is one event a day most obviously suitable for network coverage. But the electoral considerations dominate: The first question is where does the candidate have to go to look for the votes he needs to win.

Deardourff expanded on this idea of the relationship between the candidate's need to reach specific voters and his desire to accommodate the networks' needs:

> Each candidate has to develop, as soon as the nominating process is over, an electoral strategy, which is going in large part to dictate the physical travel and also the issue content of the campaign.

> But once having done that, and once having decided where the votes have to come from and what kind of issues are vote productive with the people who have to be influenced, then you begin to take into account how then do you communicate those issues, and that's where this dance begins with the media.

Deardourff also stressed the need to accommodate the needs of local television outlets; the candidate goes to those places where he needs to get the votes, but he goes at those times and under those circumstances to maximize the opportunity for getting television coverage. Morton and Woodruff agreed that the candidate has a good chance at scheduling himself so that whatever he wants to have on the nightly news will be covered. Sometimes, they said, the network correspondents have the opportunity to stand back and do a daily piece with some perspective; and sometimes a question at the airport will elicit a spontaneous response from the candidate that will be more newsworthy than the event he wants to be covered.

Gralnick noted that there is nothing new about scheduling the candidate to meet the needs of the media; it's just that it used to be done for the a.m. and p.m. cycles of the newspapers and now it is for television.

Schmidt asked Gralnick about the extent of the effort to do so-called enterprise reporting, that is, stories that develop original information and go beyond what Gralnick called "here they come and there they go" pieces. Gralnick described the allocation of effort to enterprise reporting this way:

> You do it as you feel a need or a sense that a given issue has become important or a given aspect of a candidate's life or personality has become important. . . . But in the continuity of evening news coverage, as a campaign perks along from September to November, you have in mind that you must do it and you pick your best possible time. . . .

> Last campaign we picked our shot two weeks before the campaign ended and said we're going to go Monday to Friday on five major issues, how do the candidates compare. In any given broadcast week we devoted over twenty-five percent of our total air time to the basic dissection of issues.

This was better, he suggested, than the *New York Times* did on its front page, but Clymer strongly disagreed.

Schmidt asked Bagdikian about the enterprise reporting on the networks vis-à-vis the newspapers. He responded by suggesting that both the print and electronic media were failing to get issues before the public that the candidates refused to talk about. To do so, he said, would require "changing forms, creating forms . . .":

> The *New York Times* can devote a double-page spread on issues, not on candidates, but issues the public are worried about, alternative solutions that various people have for it, and it doesn't cost them much.

> If the networks did it properly, which I think they ought to, it might take them four prime time hours during the campaign, not about the candidates, but what the issues are, and what alternative solutions are being offered by various people. But that would mean that they would have to give up a lot of money. The newspapers don't have to give up that kind of money.

"They also wouldn't have much of an audience," Deardourff added. Deardourff went on to compliment Gralnick and ABC on the issues coverage

Gralnick referred to earlier, stressing that seeing the candidates' positions without "a lot of editorial comment about why they took those positions or where they took them" was "a substantial step forward from previous campaign coverages." He suggested that packaging such information into the nightly news was a much more effective way of reaching many more people than doing special programs on the issues that would command a much smaller audience.

Deardourff's expressions of interest in coverage of issues again ran headlong into the skepticism of the networks about what coverage the candidates really wanted during the campaign. Martin Plissner spoke first:

> There seems to be a notion around here that a political candidate as he goes around the country is expounding day after day on a variety of new issues and taking new positions which we're failing to report. This isn't really what happens. . . .
>
> The candidate that goes from one town to another, arranging to get his sound bites on one television station or the other, is saying substantially the same thing one place or another. Occasionally he says something reportable, because he does adopt a new and interesting position, or he does say something crazy. . . . But we do not normally have an issue kind of campaign for the Presidency, and what we are reporting is a fair reflection of what is happening out there.

To Morton, people do not vote on issues. They "vote on character," he said, "the kind of person that they like."

Election Night

Schmidt began the discussion of election-night coverage by asking Leonard about the use of exit polls that result in projecting a winner before the polls have closed. Here is Leonard's response:

> It is not true that our exit polling or our analysis has a demonstrable effect. . . . It hasn't been true now for twenty-five years, and there have been all kinds of attempts to make that case. . . .
>
> We are in the business of doing a very simple thing, and I think it is a highly responsible thing. . . . How it got fast and how it got sophisticated is in reference to that very simple thing. And that is, to tell people what the wire services before us have attempted to tell people, what the *Times*, the *Daily News*, the *Los Angeles Times*, what any responsible journalistic organization is trying to do, and that is to tell them the very simple and most important decision that the American people can know, who is going to be the next President of the United States.
>
> Now, it seems to us very clear that this is an important piece of information. It is a piece of information that, if we have, we shouldn't withold, and it is a

piece of information that is worth a great deal of effort on our part to try to find out.

And that is the basis, simple as that, of the three networks' enormous efforts to determine who has won on election night.

Schmidt asked him whether he would be concerned if the early forecasting of results did affect the outcome of, for instance, a statewide race in California. Leonard responded:

> Yes, it would worry me. . . . I do not think it is incumbent on reporters to provide the solution. The problem is a geographic one; . . . if this is an important question and demonstrably needs to be solved at the federal level, it should be solved at the federal level. It should not be solved by abrogating the First Amendment.

Clymer suggested that the uniform twenty-four-hour voting period would be the simplest way of addressing the problem, but it would not solve it. "Networks are broadcasting before the polls have closed anyway," he said, and they would just stop a little short of saying that someone had been elected. However, Clymer cautioned against federal regulation, preferring to see the networks regulate themselves to prevent an early call of a race demonstrably influencing the outcome of other contests.

Ridings raised the more basic issue: That it is not possible to prove that exit polls do damage does not mean they should be used. "What public policy does it serve?" she asked.

Warren Mitofsky defended the use of exit polls and projections generated by them. He noted that such projections are made on a state-by-state basis and broadcast only after the polls have closed in that state; the networks have declined to make projections in an individual state before the polls closed even though the technology and the knowledge were available to do so.

Reynolds responded to Ridings:

> I don't have any qualms about it. . . . I am not at all sure that it is the function of the journalistic establishment in this country to set public policy, and I'm not sure that Ms. Ridings' question is exactly pertinent.

Reynolds's comment generated a brief intense exchange between him and Edward Diamond on the broader questions of journalistic responsibility and network-politician relations. First Diamond: "When I heard Mr. Reynolds talking, it reminded me of Tom Lerher's lyric about Werner von Braun and his rockets, 'I only send them up; I don't care where they come down.' " Then Reynolds: "Our business is to publish, not to supress." Then Diamond again:

As I listened to the discussion this morning, what I saw were two television wrestlers, the campaign on the one hand, the press on the other. They know each other's moves, they've grappled with each other before, and it makes a helluva show.

Afterword

In retrospect, perhaps Diamond's closing remark framed the central theme of the morning. The session was designed to identify and highlight the issues of conflict between the networks and the politicians; but more than anything else, it demonstrated how much in sync the two forces seemed to be. They need each other, rely on each other, meet each other's needs. The candidates' handlers talked about their willingness to accommodate their campaigns to the constraints faced by the networks. And for the most part, the networks disdained any independent responsibility for the shape and flow of the electoral process even as the politicians were acknowledging how large a role in their decision making television did play.

When the politicians and the networks sensed a shared view around the table that the product of their independent activity was not working out in the public interest, they were each quick to place the blame on the other. Do the networks overcover the early primaries because the candidates spend so much time and money on them? Or do the candidates spend so much time and money on them because the networks are going to be there in force? Or, to take another example, do the campaigns and candidates seem relatively without substance because that is the way the candidates want it? Or, does the coverage dwell on the horse-race rather than the policies because horse-race coverage fits in well with the conventions and demands of the networks' nightly news programs?

In two instances, one factor on the press side—the competitiveness among the networks—seems to skew news judgment or, better, campaign-coverage judgment. First was the decision to follow one another into the early-primary states and into the conventions. And second was the pressure to be first in announcing winners on election night.

Real conflict did surface between the networks and the regulatory system on two accounts, foreshadowing the discussion to be held on the regulatory issues on Sunday morning. First, the networks were concerned about the impact of the Supreme Court decision affirming the ruling of the Federal Communications Commission that the networks had violated the reasonable access requirement when they refused to sell a half-hour of prime time to the Carter-Mondale Committee in early December 1979. They see the result as taking away some of their proper editorial discretion as to when to start accepting political advertisements. Their objections to the decision were based on both free press and commercial grounds. Second, there was widespread dissatisfaction, shared by many of the nonnetwork people sitting around the table, with the restrained role for the networks imposed by the current interpretation of the equal-opportunities/equal-time law as it is applied to candidate debates. It should be noted, however, that on both these questions the dispute is between the networks and the regulatory apparatus, not between the networks and the politicians directly, although the politicians, at least those in Congress, could solve the networks' problems on both these scores.

To be sure, there were some differences between the networks and the politicians. The candidates want to set the issue agenda; the networks want to play a somewhat independent role, adding items to the agenda that the politicians have not addressed. The candidates want their message out exactly as they deliver it; the networks feel a responsibility to the viewers of explaining the message and surrounding it with the political context in which it is taking place. The candidates expressed a strong interest in buying prime time in chunks that would suit their needs; the networks said that accommodating candidates' demands for length and time of day would be extremely disruptive to their scheduling practices.

But these were hardly the differences of bitter rivals in a so-called adversarial relationship between the press and the politicians. The differences, such as they seemed to be, were all within a broader context of shared values and experiences. Everyone around the table was, as Richard E. Neustadt characterized them (including himself), a "political junkie" who, as Small remarked, was "hungry to get into the game." When they disagreed, at least at this stage, it was on matters of professional perspective and self-interest, not basic principle or the public's need for a certain kind of election process.

4 The Networks Look at Themselves

Major Dramatis Personae (in Order of Appearance)

Floyd Abrams, Moderator, Partner, Cahill, Gordon and Reindel

George Reedy, Nieman Professor of Journalism, Marquette University

Bruce Morton, Correspondent, CBS News

Judy Woodruff, White House Correspondent, NBC News

Harold Bruno, Jr., Director of Political Coverage, ABC News

Tom Brokaw, News Correspondent, NBC News

William Leonard, President, CBS News

Richard Wald, Senior Vice-President, ABC News

Michael J. Robinson, Director, Media Analysis Project, George Washington University

Jeffrey Gralnick, Vice-President and Executive Producer, Special Events, ABC News

Roger Mudd, Chief Washington Correspondent, NBC News

Elizabeth Drew, Journalist

Robert MacNeil, Executive Editor, The MacNeil-Lehrer Report

Adam Clymer, Political Correspondent, *New York Times*

Martin Plissner, Political Director, CBS News

Frank Reynolds, Chief Anchor, World News Tonight, ABC News

John D. Deardourff, Chairman of the Board, Bailey, Deardourff, and Associates

Dot Ridings, First Vice-President and Communications Chair, League of Women Voters of the United States

Edwin Diamond, Editorial Director, *Ad Week*

Frank Stanton, Retired President, CBS Inc.

Richard S. Salant, Former President, CBS News

F. Christopher Arterton, Associate Professor of Political Science, Yale University

Richard E. Neustadt, Professor of Public Administration, John F. Kennedy School of Government

Gary Orren, Associate Professor of Public Policy, John F. Kennedy School of Government

The first session on Saturday afternoon was designed to explore the problems of covering the presidential elections from the networks' perspectives. Among the issues to be examined were the constraints imposed on coverage by the limitations and demands of the technology of television itself and the degree to which the candidates were able to control the flow of news.

Moderator Floyd Abrams opened the discussion by announcing that he wanted to dispense with the question-and-answer, dialogue format and give the network people, "in a somewhat more discoursive and reflective way," the opportunity to share their concerns and their frustrations with the present terms and conditions imposed on television election coverage. He began by using a hypothetical case about an incumbent president's deciding that he would not seek reelection. The purpose, he said, was to try to get at how the networks would respond, whom they would seek out, and how they would determine who the real candidates were.

The Networks as Candidate Makers

Just before asking for comment, Abrams sharpened the focus of the hypothetical by asking participants to assume that a year before his term was up, President Reagan announced on television, without warning, that he had decided not to run. The question on the floor for the networks then became, in Abrams's words, "who, the next morning on your shows and that night, if you had a chance to think it out after the President spoke, would you in the ordinary course of your journalistic judgment be listing . . . as potential candidates?" Among those the participants mentioned were Vice-President George Bush, Senator Howard Baker, Congressman Jack Kemp, Alexander Haig, Senator Jesse Helms, and Senator Robert Dole.

Some participants began to question the hypothetical case, suggesting that President Reagan would already have someone in place if he were to make such an announcement (George Reedy), or that he would never make such an announcement with as much as a year left in his term (Gerald

Rafshoon). Abrams wondered whether and how those potential candidates would get themselves on television. Bruce Morton suggested several different ways and noted that "in that climate, the press would follow along and pay attention." Judy Woodruff and Stuart Loory argued that the candidates would not have to do anything because the networks would be seeking them out. And Reedy added that the candidates would be more interested in looking for financial support and delegate commitments than in getting on television right after the announcement.

Abrams asked the participants to describe the decision-making process that would take place at the networks after such an announcement. What he seemed to be looking for was the degree to which the networks would make decisions about which potential candidates would be taken seriously and which would not. Bruno responded:

There really isn't that much decision making. . . .

So much of it are decisions that are in effect made for you by the flow of the news. If something like this were to happen, the news would be so obvious. For example, you would want to go to the Democratic Party because suddenly their nomination would be worth a lot more than it was going against an incumbent president. . . .

What you think is decision making, what the outside world thinks is decision making, really isn't at all. It is going the way the news is going. . . .

Ben Bagdikian narrowed the focus. He suggested that there is a "hierarchy of political reporting" and that the ones at the top of the hierarchy would have columns and commentary about potential candidates that would "tend to crystallize" other journalists' thinking about certain people. Tom Brokaw pointed out that even for those trend-setting journalists, the process of deciding whom to focus on would be an evolutionary one. These journalists too would be on the telephone, taking soundings, assessing the polls.

Abrams then asked the question that he had been skirting around until then: Just how much of an independent player is television news in the process of sorting out who would be the leading candidates for president?

Brokaw said that television news "obviously" would be a player but that it would be more so in the morning programs than in the evening-news shows. In the morning there would be "some fermentation that takes place in terms of discussion" rather than the "kind of passing parade of names in the evening." David Gergen noted that the speculative process takes place much earlier in print than in the electronic press. William Leonard agreed and suggested why it was so:

I wouldn't underestimate the influences of the regular print press on the shaping of the thoughts and exchanges that go on in the television and the radio.

They are very easily available. It is awfully easy to read everything that is written politically in the *New York Times* and the *Washington Post*, for instance, even easier than it is to watch everything that is done on your [network] opposition.

Richard Wald suggested that the political consultants ought to be added to the list of those who have a role in the sifting-out process. They are neither independent observers nor actual participants, he said, but "they are part of the developing sense" of things. They are the kinds of people who would be consulted by the networks for intelligence and information on what was happening.

Michael Robinson concluded this segment of the session by wondering whether the participants evidenced a Washington bias in suggesting who would be the likely candidate, which therefore slighted governors as potential national leaders.

The Networks Bare Their Souls

Abrams then turned the discussion to his primary focus for the rest of the session: "I would like to start a dialogue, now, about what you think the most real, most serious, most pervasive problems are in your ability to do the job as well as you would like to be able to do it."

Wald was the first to respond:

People don't watch what we do when we do what we say we are most interested in doing. The history of both conventions and elections is that decreasing numbers of people watch, in terms of the ratings.

We are people whose own internal juices flow and motors go in terms of covering politics, and we get all geared up and we spend two years in preparing for a convention. All three of us go there, and more or less, certainly this past time, all three of us cover gavel to gavel, and more and more people stay away.

Local movies get more viewers than the conventions do. Something is wrong. There is a problem here. We think of it as important and as interesting, but the country, to a growing degree, doesn't. We think of it as being a linchpin of democracy, but the country thinks of it as a bore.

Election night comes around, and we are going to elect the most important elected official in the western world, unless Mrs. Gandhi is going to be elected or appointed again, and people decreasingly watch. . . .

I think that we have a problem. We invest a lot of effort, ingenuity, interest, money, machinery, sweat into this thing, and we don't seem to be doing the thing we say we're doing. There is a discontinuity between what our perception of what we are doing is and the reality of what happens. . . .

Somewhere in that question of horse race, personalities, and issues, we have become decreasingly connected with the people of this country. We are not, except occasionally, speaking to the issues that engage them, and we become overly concerned with issues that engage the most vocal and active of them to the neglect of issues that engage the least vocal and least active.

We vote less and less, and there is a connection between the amount we vote and the amount we watch. And I think it is a problem—of course I think of it as a problem of the politicians and not of the journalists, but I think it is a problem for both of us. And it is a problem of a nature that seems to me not merely bad, but antidemocratic, because we keep making rules, the FCC keeps helping us not to put things on the air, and we keep making rules that seem to narrow what it is we can do.

I'll give you one instance only. During an election campaign, it would be useful to have a program on the air once a week, half an hour, an hour of prime time, fringe time—leave that aside for the moment—that would summarize the campaign. But you can't do it, because it isn't sensible to do it unless you can show the candidates, and you can't show the candidates, and you can't show the candidates because of Section 315. If you do it without the candidates, it looks silly, and there are all sorts of problems.

Abrams wondered whether the networks would really invest in such a program if there were no Section 315. Wald responded:

We did it once; . . . there was produced a program that was half an hour long, in prime time, that would deal only with the politics of the week. And because of the rules, it would not involve any of the candidates for office.

The program appeared twice, and it was so terrible, because you were always saying, "well, George said," but you can't show George. . . . It wasn't interesting. Nobody watched it.

Stephen Sharp felt that the discussion of what the networks would do without the current broadcast regulations was particularly important as policymakers begin to decide whether or not to keep those rules as they are. He wondered whether the present lack of viewer interest in some aspects of political coverage would change if the coverage were different or whether the disinterest was attributable to the political process regardless of what the networks did.

Abrams asked for some reaction to the fact of falling viewership for convention and election-night coverage and to Sharp's question of where the responsibility for that fact lay. Jeffrey Gralnick responded, and his comments began one of the most revealing introspective dialogues of the conference. For Gralnick, the shrinking audience for network campaign coverage was an issue primarily for the political process:

I don't think it is television's problem. Yes, audiences for convention coverage, audiences for election coverage have fallen, and they have fallen, some of the studies indicate, in lock step with the decrease in the number of people who vote. Fewer people are interested in voting. Therefore, fewer people are interested in watching to find out about the results.

I think that there might be a problem with politics or politicians. And Jerry [Rafshoon] was sitting here saying that the politicians aren't any better or worse today than they were four years ago, eight years ago, twelve years ago; maybe it is just that we are holding up a mirror to them and letting more people see what they really are.

Yes, we four networks collectively would like everybody on election night to sit down and watch election coverage. That is unthinkable, because only half the people voted. Therefore, half the people don't even want to know about the process, the politics, or who is being elected, because half the people don't think it matters.

I think there may be a problem with the political process and the candidates that the parties are pushing forward, rather than with the coverage of what is out there to cover.

Roger Mudd disagreed and made a powerful statement for accepting some responsibility for disenchantment with politics:

For me, the basic problem is the conflict between being an honest reporter and being a member of show business, and that conflict is with me every day. If you are dedicated to honest, unaffected untrammeled reporting, you run up against the demands of making the news that evening interesting.

I think over the last fifteen years, as competition has sharpened between the networks, none of us is content to let an event be an event; we have to fix it. We have to foreshorten the conclusions; we have to hasten the end. We have to predict, before anybody else knows, who is going to win. We have to take an issue. We won't let the candidate lay out the issue on his own terms; he has to lay it out on our terms. We have to take quantels and chyrons and spinning cubes to make the issues interesting.

For me, it is a daily dilemma, and I think sometimes, at three o'clock in the morning, that maybe we give people too much, and that's why they don't watch.

Leonard noted his agreement with "a great deal" of what Mudd had to say. Then he expanded on Mudd's remarks, laying out his views of the ways in which the constraints of television and the business of networks have affected political coverage:

I feel in some sense we in television, in broadcast journalism, are a little bit trapped, and that subconscious of it or conscious of it, we are serious people who try to practice this trade almost every day.

In the first place, we're trapped by our own origins and trapped in the sense that we are very young, only twenty-five years old, and we're trapped by origins which came from print, and we're not sure just where we fit in in relation to that. We're a little bit trapped by our origins from radio. We don't know quite whether we're a form of print translated via radio into pictures, or a form of pictures that come from radio—we don't yet quite know who and what we are in television.

Secondly, I think we are trapped, to a degree, by competition. Competition has been responsible for a great many extraordinary advances in the work of networks and network broadcast journalistic efforts, not the least of which is the way we cover election night in and not the least of which is the way, in the past, at least, we have covered conventions.

But to some degree, it has led to a distortion of what we do. We cannot help being conscious of our circulation, and occasionally, we are almost solely conscious of our circulation. There would be no discussion, none whatsoever, of whether we continued to cover the conventions gavel to gavel, if the number of viewers, that is, our circulation, was high or as high as it used to be.

Third, I think we're also trapped, and other people have made this point, by the very nature of the business that we are in. We exist in between the pages of a business—this point was made by Dr. Ward last night, and there is nothing original about it—but we do exist between the pages of a business that is primarily successful because it is the greatest means of mass medium entertainment ever invented.

105 million people, one out of every two people in the United States, watched the entertainment of the Super Bowl. That is fundamentally what the business is all about, and it is fundamentally what supports most of it. We exist alternately with that. We are confused with that, and sometimes we are confused by that.

I think it is a tribute, actually, to the management of all three networks that they have insisted, over all this quarter of a century, that we are important, that we be allowed to flourish, that we be given the resources to flourish; but nevertheless, it is a confusion.

Finally, one final point, I think we are trapped a little bit by not our failures but by our success. And perhaps this is the most dangerous point of all for the future. At the local level, we are simply the most important single factor in the success of 1,000 television stations, the news. The financial health of those stations depends on their circulation and their coverage of the news; and the word, the emphasis, is circulation.

In the last ten years, we have seen the development where news was no longer a loss leader or something we did for the FCC or something we did for prestige or something we did because we felt we ought to do it or because we felt good about doing it or because it was something for the commonweal.

All over the country it is something that must be done, because if you don't do it and don't do it successfully, you are going to go out of business. And now we're beginning to see that at the network level. The dollars are very, very large. There is nothing wrong with that.

The single most successful broadcast in the history of television is not a fictional program, but nonfiction, "*60 Minutes*." In the very success that we enjoy lie the real problems that we have to grapple with in the future.

The Bad-News Business

With the opening provided by Mudd and Leonard, others began to discuss specific problems of network coverage of the election process. Elizabeth Drew picked up Wald's comments about the networks' losing their audience for coverage of the campaigns and elections:

> I think maybe there is a saturation problem. I don't think there are any charts or graphs on the amount of time that goes into coverage now that there are so many primaries and caucuses—if that has grown.

> I think that there may be something to that, also a failure to make a distinction between what is important and what is not important. There is gearing up for the X primary or caucus; even if it turns out not to matter very much, there it is. So it is a kind of one-dimensional approach. And it is there every week.

> We all know we need not go into the history of Vietnam and Watergate and all that. But obviously other things have gone on in the body politic that do have to do with people's reaction to politicians and cynicism and distrust of what they say. That is not a function of the political coverage of campaigns. It is there as part of our history, and the recovery or not from that is a separate matter.

> Then, to bring up one more point that is a very delicate one—and I do it with some misgivings—I wonder to what extent the tone with which we cover campaigns affects the public's reaction to it. Politicians are far from perfect, and I believe very strongly in being skeptical about them, and, when they say things that are wrong, correcting them—raising questions about what they say.

> I certainly don't think we should be humorless in our approach to the comedy and absurdity of campaigns. But I wonder if sometimes the sum total of the coverage doesn't tip over to the point where the process is robbed of any sense of majesty, inspiration, where it does become very heavily an approach that runs down just about everybody who tries to get into it.

> We could analyze why this happens to whatever degree it does happen. But the poor soul who straggles across that finish line, to the extent they make it, has been pretty bloodied by the time he gets there.

> Again, it is a tough thing to draw, but I wonder if we haven't had some effect on the public's reaction, which is, "To the extent I care, they are all a bunch of bums and fools."

Although she was not referring to network coverage alone, Drew had raised a sensitive subject. The questions of whether network political coverage was unfairly negative and whether that negativeness contributed to other problems in the body politic were not new but were issues with which the network people were concerned. Abrams asked whether participants thought that cynicism toward politicians was peculiar to television coverage or whether it reflected attitudes in print journalism and in society at large. Robert MacNeil thought they were problems unique in the electronic medium:

It is more on television, and there is a reason why it is more on television. I'm not absolutely on sure ground, but I think that television has had in its political reporting a kind of historical inferiority complex. . . .

Television political reporting, with apologies and deference to the very skilled political reporters who are here, has always been to a large degree derivative of what is in the print press. I know television makes its original contributions, but a lot of the value judgments and a lot of the feel comes from the more extensive work that full-time political reporters on the principal newspapers and the wire services are able to do.

That's one thing, and I think that as a result of this inferiority complex relative to print, television political reporters feel they have to express their detachment and distance from the material, even more aggressively, perhaps, especially as they are given such an exceedingly brief amount of time, usually two sentences at the end of the piece, which is, after all, their face, their by-line, their career involvement every night.

This was commented on in a very interesting column during the last campaign, that it had reached a point where this columnist alleged that there was almost a competition in bitchiness.

This is not original to the 1980 campaign. I could say that I felt this myself as far back as the middle sixties, that the exceedingly brief amount of time available to you as a television reporter, taking great pride in the professionalism with which you can put together the sort of little mini-mini-documentary that your piece of one minute thirty is, and have it relatively accurate in terms of what you think the sense of that day's campaign was or the themes that have been evolving, to be able to express yourself at all, your individuality, your presence, and your cynicism, if you like, or your sophistication about politics, that inclines you to compress into very few words what, I think, could easily be interpreted as cynicism, and a generally sour or sort of—I can't think of the right word—tone of disparagement. . . .

One wide point is, has television's political coverage evolved from a basis, in each form of it, as television sitting down and thinking, "How can we be of service to the voters of this country," or has it evolved in forms that have suited the convenience of television as an emerging industry? Were the conventions covered and did the coverage evolve as it has done because it might be useful for the voters, or has it evolved because of the person who thinks it will sell television sets and so on? That's one point, and I think you could trace that through the nightly news and the other forms that are used.

Often I find television bewilderingly compressed and difficult to follow and dealing on a level of sophistication, I think, way above many voters.

The other point is, apart from the factors that Liz [Drew] mentioned of the alienation from politicians that may be traceable from Watergate and Vietnam and so on, there has also been a growing cheapening of the political process, in my view, by the continued and increasing resort to brief commercial messages as one of the principal means of communicating political messages.

I personally think that should be outlawed in this country. I know you can't do it, but I think it should be outlawed. If you are going to reduce the political dialogue to the equivalent of commercials for a deodorant or whatever—because I think the public is very cynical about all of that and quite understands what is being done to it when it is being sold consumer goods—I think you cannot help but have a kind of low level, accumulative, intuitive disparagement of politics and a cheapening of politics through that.

In between his two concluding points, MacNeil had suggested that the "level of sophistication" of political reporting on television might be "way above many voters." Mudd identified with that idea and recounted a rather startling anecdote that provided some dramatic confirmation of the notion that network correspondents and anchors were talking about political campaigns as insiders in coded language that would be fully intelligible only to fellow political insiders. Mudd recounted his experience during the 1980 presidential election campaign when he was "between networks" and spent the political season as a consumer, rather than as a deliverer, of television news:

As my well of information dried up, because I was not going to work every day, . . . my active crackling facts diminished. So I began to watch television in the evening and the morning, as most consumers would, men and women who read the paper and hear things around the neighborhood and the grocery store but really weren't plugged in.

As the campaign went on, as I tried to keep up, I found myself unable to understand half of what I was hearing on the nightly news. I did not bring with me enough first class, up-to-date information to understand what was going on. There were so many pieces of shorthand built into the switch to Des Moines, the tightly edited clip, the voice left up in the air telling me that the guy had been cut short, that when the evening news was over, I felt unsatisfied and dissatisfied and not very proud, and not very well informed.

Abrams asked him whether he agreed with the comments by Drew and MacNeil that suggested that there is a kind of "continuing, subliminal, sometimes overt disparagement of the political process" by the manner in which American news is presented. Mudd explained that

if I had given four days of my life to covering a candidate from South Dakota to Texas to Georgia, and on Thursday I'm expected to do a piece about that week and that candidate and that campaign, I don't want that piece to end up with the nation thinking I'm a fool, and that something has been put over on me. And you're damn right I'm going to try to be sophisticated and smart. . . .

Photo by Martha Stewart

Left to right: David Gergen, Assistant to the President for Communications, The White House; Robert MacNeil, Executive Editor, The MacNeil-Lehrer Report; Roger Mudd, Chief Washington Correspondent, NBC News; Michael Robinson, Director Media Analysis Project, George Washington University; and Irwin Segelstein, Vice Chairman of the Board, NBC Inc.

But, Mudd concluded, that process "becomes pernicious."

Robinson spoke next and used the opportunity to discuss findings from his comprehensive study comparing print and electronic coverage of the 1980 presidential election:

> The reason that we got involved in this study . . . is that I had a supposition that tone on television was different from the tone in journalism that used to give most Americans their coverage of the campaign, which is to say the wires through the local press. So what this whole study was, basically, was built on testing the notion that television would be more critical if not more cynical in its approach to politicians. . . . We used CBS and we used UPI, and we started in January and went through December. . . .
>
> Eighty percent of the stories in both sources were neither good press nor bad press, which is to say they were right down the middle, as most of the people in television I'm sure can understand. They offered no coloration really about the candidate.
>
> Among the twenty percent on CBS and UPI that did have coloration, the ratio of good press to bad on the wire was three to two positive. On television, CBS, the ratio was four to one negative. . . . So we have a fairly positive image of the candidates on the wire, a fairly negative image of the candidates on CBS. In fact, every candidate who received coverage in both media was treated more critically on CBS than the wire. . . .
>
> In 1980, people had a negative perception of both candidates in the first time in a national survey. While one could make a case that this is a function of having moved from traditional print to network television, I don't know if I would be willing to conclude that television therefore has alienated the population from its political leadership, and therefore it is television journalism with its cynicism or its tone that is responsible.
>
> What I think has probably happened here is that television is more critical or more cynical or more negative in its coverage of political leadership, especially candidates, than traditional print; but what you have really got going on in the last few years is that those people who never really thought about candidates before, who just showed up as Democrats or showed up as Republicans, have now seen a relatively unflattering view of candidates, and they are not voting. But that is a different thing from saying that there has been a broad-based alienation from people of all sorts in the political process.
>
> One thing that we found in this study was that if you look at the amount of people who come to Washington to talk to their representatives about public policy, between 1970 and 1980, that's increased by a factor of three.
>
> Now, I'm not sure which is the sign of health or which is the sign of unhealth, but it seems to me it is clear that network television is more critical of political authority than the system it replaced (which is traditional print, not the prestige press, because the *Post* and the *Times* are critical of political authority) and that there have been implications of that for the body politic. But it goes too far to say that the alienation of the political process is the fault of network television.

It may well be that soon enough down the line, network television will produce some relatively favorable consequences for mass-based politics.

Robinson's conclusions were challenging to the networks, and Bruno was the first to take issue with him:

I have had the experience of covering national politics for a newspaper, a national news magazine, and now for radio and television, and I think what is sometimes mistaken for a critical attitude on the part of the television correspondent really isn't that at all.

Many of the political reporters in the national scene for whom we have the greatest respect in print have the advantage of being able to make use of not-for-attribution material. When the candidate is being interviewed, and he comes out with a self-serving platitude, you can come back in print and say, "However, aides said, or other unidentified people said that it isn't quite the way the candidate says."

I, for one, see nothing wrong with a professional television political correspondent being able to go on camera and to wind up the piece that he or she does with some intellectual depth perception that tells people, "Look, here is what he says, but on the other hand, here is what we have learned in talking to people and in doing our job as reporters."

I don't see why the broadcast media cannot have that same privilege.

Bruno's defense generated responses from others. It was, perhaps, the first time during the conference when the network people and the non-network participants were on opposite sides of an extended exchange. The issue of negative coverage carried strong feelings on both sides. Adam Clymer was the first to answer Bruno:

The smart-aleck close is something that is used by a lot of people who are not professional political reporters on television. It is a device with which one copes with a very short piece, trying to prove to the country that you haven't been fooled; and it is not something which is quite as thoughtful as the way you described it just now.

There is one other point about the negative voice of television on politics. The political commentator in the United States who has by all odds the biggest audience is uniformly negative on politics. That's Johnny Carson. Carson consistently treats politicians as bumblers and fools; he's very entertaining, and he has a bigger audience than anyone else who does political commentary.

Reedy was doubtful that television's style and tone of coverage had negatively affected politics:

I just want to put in a sort of cautionary note about the assumption that because television capsulizes things and brings them down to simple slogans that it has somehow done something to our politics. . . .

I remember a senator from North Carolina who was . . . successful on the campaign slogan, "Do you want that man in the Senate who eats fish eggs from Red Soviet Russia, or a boy that eats good old North Carolina hen eggs?" And I somehow just don't think that whatever the sins of television are, and they may be considerable, that they really have affected American politics in that sense. I think that this is just a new device for carrying on something that is rather old.

Martin Plissner added another word of caution about speculation on the causal relationship between negative network political coverage and low voter turnout. He pointed out that while turnout has gone down in the last three elections, it has decreased so slightly that "it would be hard to draw many conclusions from it as to its source, or even be an interesting matter of inquiry." Furthermore, he added, during the early 1980 caucuses and primaries, the period of the "savaging of the participants," turnout was way up over the similar period in 1976.

Woodruff tried to turn the conversation away from what she characterized as "self-flagellation" in order to suggest "a couple of things that I think television does well." First, she said,

> we do give the public a real life image of the candidate, a much closer image than they can get from reading a news magazine or reading a newspaper. You can argue about whether that is the real man or woman that is coming through, but I think that there is some value in seeing that person talking in person on the screen, even if it is just for a few seconds at night, and I think that is one thing we have been able to provide.

> I think the other thing is that we provide an accountability. It is very difficult now for a candidate to say one thing in Washington and something else in Peoria. He has got to say pretty much the same thing everywhere he goes, or he is going to be in a lot of trouble with all of the press, not just the network reporters who are covering him. And I think that accountability is a contribution that the networks have made.

Having raised her positive points, Woodruff went on to discuss one aspect of network campaign coverage that did present a problem for her:

> It does bother me that we get caught up as we do in covering the daily schedule of the candidate. We are trapped in the fact that we have to follow the candidate everywhere he goes, to every speech, to every appearance, and to some extent I think we are prisoners of his schedule.

Joan Richman, Frank Reynolds, and others agreed that this was so because of the possibility of an assassination attempt. Reynolds used the opportunity of acknowledging the death-watch aspect of campaign coverage to bring the discussion back to the charge of negativism and then to move it ahead by throwing the challenge of accountability and responsibility back at the politicians.

Frank Reynolds, Chief Anchor, World News Tonight, ABC News; and Congressman David Obey, D-Wisconsin.

Photo by Martha Stewart

The Politicians Join In

With respect to the "sour and sardonic attitude with which reporters approach their task," Reynolds said:

> Anyone who has covered a political campaign day in and day out finds it difficult, I suppose, not to loathe the candidate as the person responsible for all the personal discomfort he has to endure.

> I would also like to make another point that I think maybe ought to be put out here. What is a political campaign? Is it not an attempt to manipulate? Here is Mr. Garth, there is Mr. Rafshoon, Mr. Deardourff and others. They are media advisors. They are media manipulators. They are trying to portray the candidate in the best possible light.

> That does not necessarily mean an automatic state of war with the correspondents who are covering the campaign, but it does mean that the correspondents, the reporters, do have to try to take that into account and maybe inject some reality into their reporting, reality that may not be at all in conformity with the image that the advisors wish to project.

> What are we to do when a candidate says, "I'm glad I'm opening my campaign here with you working men and women, rather than down there where the Ku Klux Klan was born. . ."? Are we just going to let that go by? What are we to do when the candidate says, "The election of my opponent would not be good for the country"? I'm merely suggesting that sometimes they are not a very lovable bunch, and it is necessary, I think, to try to be objective and detached, but it is also very important not to be taken in.

David Garth agreed that, in Abrams's words, "One of the functions of a good reporter is not to be taken in" by candidates and their consultants. But Garth went on to suggest that criticism from reporters was fair as long as the candidates did have the opportunity also to get their messages across unfettered:

> One of the problems is that the candidates have no other way to reach the public, unfortunately, except by thirty-second spots (you can't really buy five minute spots or get them for nothing); . . . every appearance that he has is an interpretation by a newspaper reporter by a television reporter of what he meant or what he said or what he stood for.

> My feeling is that there ought to be the criticism, and that a candidate ought to have a chance, at least for two minutes a day, to get his message out. Then they can tear him apart if they want. Unfortunately, you can't buy two-minute spots or five minute spots or any other spots, except for thirty-second spots.

John Deardourff did not agree that the "smart aleck close" was a serious general problem, although he did say that it became habitual with some reporters. More important to him was Garth's complaint about the difficulty in transmitting the views of the candidate "as he or she wishes to express them." Deardourff pointed out that it was not the candidates or their media advisors who choose to use the thirty-second commercial:

That is what we are forced to use.

It is not that we would not like to have longer segments. It is not that we would not like to be in the prime viewing time with the precise words of candidates. That simply is not an option. We heard it reaffirmed this morning that that just wasn't in the nature of the television business.

I don't know why it isn't, frankly. They sell more than six minutes of commercial time in most hour segments; why can't we have five of those six? They don't want it packaged that way.

The programming is packaged the way they want it packaged. In 1976, when they wanted to do it, they simply made a decision six months ahead of time that they would produce twenty-five-minute programs.

They have complete control. They write them. They produce them. All they have to decide is that instead of a twenty-five- or twenty-six-minute program they are going to have a twenty-three-minute program. The soap opera just becomes two minutes shorter. But they're finding it difficult to do that, so we're thrown back to the thirty-second commercial.

I'm happy to have those; if we didn't, we would have nothing. We would have absolutely no way to communicate directly to the voter.

Garth jumped in, suggesting that the way candidates' programs and proposals were treated on the news programs was even worse than the thirty-second spot:

What about a program you have worked for three months on, put in hours, and the network gives you a minute and ten seconds with a sarcastic flip at the end that doesn't have any depth to it, any content to it. . . . The networks and the people who do what we do have the same problems. The time limitation just holds us up and it makes their criticism less incisive.

Abrams asked Rafshoon whether he agreed with the frustrations expressed by Deardourff and Garth. He echoed their views from his own experience:

The rules are set by the networks on how the candidates are going to present their candidacy: whether they are going to have X amount of thirty-second spots, sixty-second spots, whether or not they can buy a half hour, when it is going to be, what are the time slots that are allotted to the candidate. . . .

My experience in two presidential campaigns in dealing with networks is that we will try—and this is the networks speaking—to accommodate you the least amount possible, the least amount we have to accommodate you.

There is still a feeling that as important as a presidential election is, it is business as usual: "The selling of spots to our commercial advertisers, whether they be for toothpaste or hygenic products, is more important to us because we are going to make more money there."

The Networks Respond

For a substantial period of time, the networks had been on the receiving end of a considerable dose of criticism, some of it coming from some of their own. At this point their side began to be heard. First was Morton:

> I don't know that it is a worse business than it was ten years ago. It seems to me that, maybe the reporting is, if anything, a little better. There are ways to display information we didn't have then. . . .

> Clearly, if the evening news were an hour, you could tell more. Clearly, if you could do more campaign specials, you could tell more. But I really do think that . . . viewers meet the candidates, and I think that the level of coverage is probably better than it was when I started out in this business. I also think that though we are sometimes smart alecks, the fact is that most political reporters like politicians. Otherwise we would cover plumbers or somebody.

Then Wald:

> I would like to take issue with everybody except Bruce [Morton]. . . .

> News . . . has become an increasing part of the network landscape. Indeed, I suspect it will become an even more increasing entry in network broadcasting. Whether we are trapped by it or not is a true question for all of us. . . .

> In network television itself, I believe . . . that our reporting has gotten better. In part it has been the sophistication of the machinery we use. I don't just mean the quantels and the dubners and whatever else; I mean also the vote collecting techniques. . . . We are more expert now in the gathering and dissemination of that information than we ever were, and there is nobody in this room who has not benefited from it.

> I want to go back to the first problem I had. . . . We have not managed to capture the people in the enthusiasm that you will hear if you talk at any length to the people in this room about the subject matter at hand. In that difference, I think there is a problem that is not television's problem, but television is part of the problem.

> I think it is absolutely true that we manage from time to time to be snotty about candidates. This theory that we control the rules is ludicrous on the face of it to anyone who has ever tried to talk to a presidential candidate or his manager at a convention or almost any other point that is important to him, when you say, "But, gee whiz, couldn't we just. . ."—"No."

Photo by Martha Stewart

Moderator Benno Schmidt, Jr., and Ronald Brown, Deputy Chairman, Democratic National Committee; Bruce Morton, Correspondent, CBS News; Richard Wald, Senior Vice President, ABC News; and Tom Brokaw, News Correspondent, NBC News.

There is a lot of exchange and interchange between us and the politicians, and it is usually good. There is basically a difference of viewpoint; they want to win, and we want to report. But I think that, no matter what else it is that we go toward, we have to recognize that we share an interest, not merely as citizens, but also because we are involved in it.

We don't cover elections and conventions for money. We don't make money at this. We don't cover it for ratings. We know it is never going to beat "Dallas." We cover it for a complex of reasons that has something to do with those things, but also for a complex of reasons that deal with "you can't be a good citizen unless you do it." Never undervalue the value of hypocrisy.

However, if we are not succeeding at drawing with us a mass of the population, it is a problem for mass communication, but it is also a problem for politicians. And I don't hear any thoughts or suggestions from the politicians on why this is so.

Dot Ridings agreed:

I don't know if it has struck anyone else as it has me how many of the problems that are shared by different segments around the table have their origins in the structure of the campaign process itself. . . .

The press goes to Iowa because Iowa is there when it is, and it goes non-stop from there. The public is cynical, because maybe they say that the press has covered so much that of course you are going to get cynical after a while. You have these short political commercials that you have to deal with because of the way the system works, and that feeds cynicism and certainly not any information to the public. . . .

Look at another country . . . for example, France, where they have short elections, no paid commercial advertising at all, and the television must give certain amounts of time at certain specified times before the election. They vote on Sunday . . . and yet they lament because they had only seventy-one percent turnout in the last election.

Edwin Diamond brought the conversation back to the networks. He argued that from the point of view of the consumer/viewer,

what you see the audience getting is very simple, three versions of reality.

There is the producer's reality, the minute-thirty items, edited in Washington or New York, with two thirty-second sound bites of the candidate. The candidate puts in an eighteen-hour day, and a minute and a half reality chosen by the network gets on the air. . . .

The second version is the media advisor's reality, the artfully crafted thirty-second or sixty-second commerical, the candidate reading the lines written for him. . . .

These are two controlled realities. The only uncontrolled reality in the campaign that the audience could see was the debates, and that thanks to the League of Women Voters.

Diamond challenged the news chiefs to use their ratings success to "tell the business side to get . . . out of your way, to give you . . . the six minutes they take out of the program for commercials." Gralnick rose to the provocation:

> Sometimes the solutions, when offered by people who do not understand or really care about the reality in which we live, just don't make it. I don't control reality. I don't adjust reality. I deal, my broadcast deals, everybody's broadcast deals with the reality of a process . . . a four-year presidential campaign.
>
> I do not send the candidate out to deliver the same speech day in and day out. Our reality, the reality we deal with, is the reality that the candidate goes through, day by day. You put it on the air, within the constraints of the amount of air time we have. To say to a network (which is, you know, heaven help us, a money making corporation) to do it another way because it would be better for your sensibilities, is absurd.

Diamond responded:

> It's not my sensibilities. The audience says they believe that the network news is accurate, seventy-one percent. At the same time, the same percentage say they don't really believe what they see on television. . . . They know that the selection process is omitting reality. . . . The business side has got to give you more space.

Leonard dismissed the idea, characterizing it by arguing that Diamond "wants us to tell our bosses to go to hell, and not edit the news."

Abrams interrupted this exchange and began to bring the session to a close by asking several people who had not spoken to offer their views on what had been said, or on the more general problem faced by the networks in covering campaigns as well as possible. He called on Frank Stanton, who agreed with those who said that the quality of television journalism had "improved immeasurably" in the past ten years. He said that his priorities, if he were still active, would be to "get equality for electronic journalism with print journalism." At the top of his list would be to repeal Section 315, the equal-opportunities provision in the communications act:

> we've got our hands tied behind us. . . . We complained about the thirty-second spots, we complained about the lack of freedom to give enough time to candidates, and I would submit that 90 percent of that is because we have got 315 on the books.
>
> It has always seemed to me that one of the great things about television is or was that the average citizen could sit in the living room with a cigarette in one hand, if necessary, and a can of beer in the other, and look the candidate in the eye the way he couldn't do it at any other place unless he sat down with a personal interview. I think we all say that if we really want to judge somebody, we want to talk with him or her on a face-to-face basis—impossible in a country our size.

But without 315 on the books, I think you could do much more of that, because you could have the longer interviews where you had an opportunity to test the character of the witness by the journalist asking the questions in the place of the person in the living room.

Richard Salant said that after listening to the discussion of the defects of television, he wondered whether "we better disinvent ourselves and do what I prefer to do anyway, read." He went on to suggest his own priorities for improving campaign coverage:

> I would add to . . . the repeal of Section 315, the hour network news. I think that one of the reasons that people may have lost interest is because when you throw things at people one after another in tiny bits and pieces, they can't get involved, they can't remember what was said, and we don't have an opportunity to make it truly interesting as distinguished from entertaining.
>
> The whole question of the hour news is an extraordinary question because it involves how helpless we in network news and indeed networks can be in the face of other power centers, including the government, including affiliates. . . .
>
> But with the repeal of 315 and an hour news, at least one can find out whether those are the kinds of obstacles we believe they are, and whether there isn't a happier future for television news.

Christopher Arterton added that whatever the defects of network election coverage, people are much better informed about the candidates and their positions on issues than in the past. He returned to the discussion of the cynicism of coverage and suggested that when the campaign managers spoke, it would be clear that the strategies of the candidates and the way they treat the electoral process was derivative of the journalists' cynicism. If anything, he said, "they were more cynical about the election process than television reporters are." Arterton theorized that the networks found it "convenient" to appear to be "more objective" by being more cynical about the candidates. But he warned that people in news ought to be thinking about that attitude and its implications; even if outsiders cannot tell the network-news managers what to do, they can at least generate some concern about the possible effects on the system of the tone of their coverage. Arterton agreed with Abrams that there may be a correlation between the cynicism of the coverage and the "bobbing and weaving" of the candidates.

Brokaw spoke of the peer pressure among journalists not to be taken in by the candidates as one key source of the cynical coverage and smart-aleck close:

> It is part of the incestuous nature of what we do.
>
> We're on the airline, we're herded onto the buses, we're taken over to Mr. Garth's setting of the day and told where our cameras will be set up. The

pool cameras have been arranged for us . . . and so on. So the way to get back is to go out there and jab him quickly right at the end, . . . get one quick shot and go. I think that's part of the problem, and I do think it is a major problem.

I also think it is a major problem that television correspondents, present company included, too often succumb to the temptation to be very judgmental at the end of that one minute and thirty seconds. . . . Our standovers come to those very tidy conclusions; and then the conclusions may change, of course, the next night, depending on our changing perceptions.

Brokaw then went back to the point Mudd had made earlier about the extent to which journalists talked on the air in a code language that was only accessible to fellow political and press insiders:

What worries me in a larger sense is the symbiotic relationship that has grown up between the campaigns and our business. . . . We were talking to each other too often during those campaigns, and we have continued to do that too often. We speak in a curious shorthand, and we get caught up. . . .

I do believe that television news is doing a far better job with every passing campaign. I do think, however, that we fall in love with the subject too much.

If we devoted as much attention to other concerns of this country and found ways to share the process with other people who we ostensibly are trying to communicate with, . . . I think we would all be better off, . . . and not just in campaign years. If we devoted the resources to the other issues that are with us as well . . . as we do to campaigns, I think we would have more credibility, and I think the country would be, if you will, engaged more with what is important.

Abrams turned to Richard E. Neustadt, who took exception to some of the conventional wisdom that had been assumed during the discussion:

One, . . . apathy is not per se bad in an electorate, in a heterogeneous, large country full of basic divisiveness. The assumption . . . that it is bad is, if I may be forgiven, a professional middle class assumption which runs right through all the professions represented here. . . . I think a good deal of apathy is a good thing among the electorate in this country, and God forbid we see it vanish. . . .

Second, the first convention I went to was pretelevison, and I learned something from it. Everybody at conventions used to hate them except the people who could get into the back rooms and the corridors. The press and the managers and the bosses had a good time. The delegates hated it. Now why should we suppose that if the nation is treated to what the delegates are treated to, the nation will love it? . . .

Third, it seems to me that there is an accident of technology that television and jets came together. . . . The . . . events that some of you talk about that make life so awful . . . would have nothing to do with television if you didn't have jets.

The other thing that strikes me is . . . in addition to getting rid of equal time requirements, . . . I would also like to get rid of or at least treble the expenditure limits. A lot of the criticism that comes from saying we can't get the candidate on the television except through the screen of reporters is because people are trying desperately not to have to pay for their coverage.

Finally, . . . there is something worrisome in the turn of people away . . . from some of these political events. But I would remind you of one other historical phenomenon: Politics, electioneering, campaigning used to be a cheap, easy available entertainment in the great old days of torchlight parades, of the train at the depot and all that. There is no reason to suppose that if you can get entertainment on television, you won't take it in lieu of politics. There is nothing in our history by which we are able to say, people used to be interested in politics because they were interested in politics and not because they didn't have anything else to do. . . .

One last thing, I notice that I got a wonderful feeling out of this today, . . I'm not the only political junkie around, . . . I do think that there is a rule of thumb, maybe . . . in the networks going beyond the newsroom that makes it okay to be on television as a comedian, or an anchorman, and express that underlying traditional American distaste for politics. . . . But to be a political junkie, that other American attitude which has never been a majority attitude as far as I know, that politics is marvelous and you can't get enough of it, that's never been altogether respectable in the professional middle classes. And as near as I can tell as a television watcher, your unofficial rule is you must try not to let your enjoyment show through.

William Small speculated about whether the phenomenon of the "me generation," where people care "far less about where society is going" than about "personal comforts" might explain more about the lack of interest in politics than television's responsibility does. And Henry Geller reiterated Diamond's earlier suggestion that the networks shorten programming during the presidential election years to allow five-minute campaign advertisements.

Finally, Abrams called on Gary Orren to provide a summing up of the session. Orren recalled Ward's message from the night before and suggested that the discussion here had underscored the "accuracy and truth of the very profound kernel of his argument." Orren cautioned against holding television responsible for the problems of the political process:

The way television behaves and the way the electoral system works, each of them reflect the basic values and conditions of society. . . .

After 1960, particularly beginning around 1964, we began to see the alarming evidence of disenchantment and cynicism, which come from problems of governance—credibility gaps, Watergate, and all the rest. This was reflected in the decline in voter turnout. And it makes sense for the people in this room to reflect the basic values, conditions, and feelings in society, which they do in the coverage.

I think the kind of sour, cynical, sometimes even contemptuous attitude of the media is really a basic mirror of where society is. Thus both the nature of television behavior and the electoral system are reflecting a third factor: the basic social condition.

Afterword

The most compelling moments of the session occurred when network correspondents and managers shared their own concerns about criticisms of their political coverage that usually are heard only from network outsiders. Before the politicos could wade in with their complaints, Mudd and Leonard and others had raised them themselves. There were discussions of the influence on the best possible political coverage of television's entertainment bias, of the competition among networks, and of the relatively recent ratings successes of the network-news programs. There was a strong sense around the table that perhaps there was too much coverage, too much politics, so that viewers were saturated, and no one could distinguish between the important and the unimportant. Whether that condition contributed to problems in the political process such as lack of activist participation and low voter turnout was disputed. Ward's caution from the night before against blaming television for conditions that were caused by forces way beyond its scope was relevant here.

There was a consensus from both network and nonnetwork people that the tone of coverage was more cynical and negative than it had to be or ought to be. There was concern that network correspondents were prisoners of the candidates' schedules, and that following the candidates around day after day, listening to the same speeches, contributed to the sourness of the coverage and the prevalence of the smart-aleck close. From the network participants there seemed to be strong support for repeal of Section 315, the equal-opportunities/equal-time law, and for going to the hour-long nightly news, although most of the politicians had not yet spoken on those subjects. But the networks resisted the idea of twisting their schedules around to accommodate the candidates' desires for prime-time availability in five-minute chunks for political commercials. It was one issue on which the networks' basic needs and desires—to report the news and to make a profit—came into direct conflict with the candidates' views on how to get their messages across in order to fulfill their basic need—to win the election.

Overall the networks came in for a good deal of criticism, some considerable amount of it self-applied. In their defense some relied on the positive aspects of coverage: the technological improvements in gathering and transmitting information, the quality of the reporting, and the intensity of television's view of candidates. Some looked to other centers of power for change: the laws, the Federal Communications Commission (FCC), the politicians, the candidates, the consultants, and the people. In the last analysis, the issues between the politicians and the networks were ones of tactics and strategy and style and tone. There was a recognition that most of the problems between them could be best explained by the differences in their jobs, not in their world view. In fact, some of the most telling dialogue of the session was over concerns that the networks and the politicians were primarily performing for and communicating with each other, a handful of powerful "political junkies," to use Neustadt's phrase, in a world that could use, in Brokaw's words, a reallocation of their "resources" to more important issues.

There were no conclusions, no consensus, no recommendations on the basic question of the session, namely, whether network presidential election coverage was serving the best interests of this society or whether it was basically serving the needs and forms of television itself. But network consciences and consciousness were on display, and the concerns of the politicians and the academics were reflected and acknowledged in the industry as well.

5 How the Managers Manage the Media

Major Dramatis Personae (in Order of Appearance)

Anthony Lewis, Moderator, Columnist, *New York Times*, and Lecturer, Harvard Law School

Richard B. Wirthlin, President, Decision/Making/Information

Gerald Rafshoon, President, Rafshoon Communications

Adam Clymer, Political Correspondent, *New York Times*

William Leonard, President, CBS News

Martin Plissner, Political Director, CBS News

Roger Mudd, Chief Washington Correspondent, NBC News

Harold Bruno, Jr., Director of Political Coverage, ABC News

Richard Wald, Senior Vice-President, ABC News

David L. Garth, President, Garth Group

David R. Gergen, Assistant to the President for Communications, The White House

Ronald H. Brown, Deputy Chairman, Democratic National Committee, Partner, Patton, Boggs & Blow

John D. Deardourff, Chairman of the Board, Bailey, Deardourff and Associates

David R. Obey, Member of U.S. House of Representatives (D-Wisconsin)

Stuart Loory, Vice-President and Managing Editor, Cable News Network

William Small, President, NBC News

New York Times columnist Anthony Lewis moderated the session designed to probe the perspective of the politicos and media managers about their relationships with the networks during the presidential campaigns. He began by looking at the role of themes and slogans in presidential elections. They have been a part of the process for a long time, he noted; what is different now is the nature and power of television, the medium that transmits those messages to the voters.

Just how does a campaign for the presidency develop, refine, and disseminate its central ideas?

Controlling the Message

Lewis asked Richard Wirthlin to discuss how the Reagan campaign created its themes and used television to convey them to the electorate. Wirthlin identified two concepts that dominated the Reagan effort:

> It appeared to us early in 1979 that the election would hinge on the issue of leadership, especially as that . . . was related to solving the major problem of the economy, namely, inflation.
>
> Reagan, I think in contrast to many presidential candidates, had a pretty well-defined position on a wide variety of issues. . . .
>
> Issues were needed and used very, very strongly in developing and reinforcing the themes, in pacing the campaign, and in giving it a thrust and a dynamic as both the primary and the general campaign started to unfold. . . .
>
> And we were also extremely concerned about the impact of the hostage situation. . . . We knew, from studies that we had done in 1978 and 1979, that foreign events, especially the kind that had the elements of the hostage situation, could not only greatly affect job rating and Presidential popularity but also vote commitment.
>
> Therefore, a secondary theme that was used in the campaign was a defensive theme, to help defuse the issue of the possible return of the hostages, say, in the middle of October, and that theme and that strategy, I think, can best be summarized in the phrase, "the October surprise."

Lewis characterized the "October surprise" theme as "spreading a kind of anticipatory cynicism about it in case it occurred." Wirthlin added that the idea was developed in May. Bill Casey and Ed Meese, two senior Reagan campaign officials at that time, began to use the term then, but "the press didn't take it very seriously at that juncture." Wirthlin said that he was told that there was a lot of poking fun at it by the media early on, but during the crucial last month of the campaign, "it did seem to take on credibility" and would have been helpful in limiting the impact of the release of the hostages on the voters' decisions in November.

Wirthlin talked about the candidate's positions on issues as important because they are "the most controllable things a candidate has." Issues solidify the themes. He used President Reagan's support for the development of the Stealth bomber as an example of a foreign-policy issue used by the

Reagan campaign to reinforce the theme "peace and strength," although he lamented that the message came through only as "strength." Thus issues provide the candidate with a measure of control, particularly in reinforcing the campaign's themes, even though the candidate cannot completely control how the media is going to handle them. He described the campaign as a "process of persuasion," with the media's playing a critical role. For the candidate, he said, the relationship with the media is "as if we are in a very small cage with a 500-pound gorilla. . . . It can kill . . . occasionally it can help you."

Lewis then asked whether one explicit aspect of the Reagan campaign strategy was to keep inquiring reporters away from the candidate and allow the messages of the campaign to be communicated as they were planned to be without being distracted by unpredictable questions and spontaneous answers.

Gerald Rafshoon said it was a good strategy and very frustrating to the Carter campaign. The Carter people asked the media covering them why they did not make an issue out of Reagan's lack of accessibility and why they did not press him on the issues President Carter was raising. But the message never penetrated, Rafshoon said, because his campaign had access only to the reporters covering them and not to the reporters covering Reagan. Only the Reagan campaign's press entourage would have been in a position to flush out the candidate.

Did the press push Reagan's campaign, both on accessibility and on the issues Carter raised? Adam Clymer said they did about as well as it is ever possible to do with that problem. He noted that there was television film showing Reagan aides shoving reporters away from the candidate, but he was not sure that people cared about candidate accessibility as an issue. Rafshoon agreed, suggesting that it was an issue only in Washington, for political insiders, particularly because there was considerable apathy among the public about the campaign in general.

Wirthlin reminded those critical of the Reagan campaign strategy that limiting access to the candidate was not unique to one campaign; Carter had his "Rose Garden strategy," following which he stayed in the White House and did not travel the campaign trail. Both sides were trying to control the images and the words that emanated from the candidate and the campaign:

> Open and free access to either Carter or Reagan enhances the probability that your campaign becomes event-driven by things you can't control. . . .

> We had to be very careful that the messages that we were sending out were very directed and very focused and very consistent and all build toward the issue of driving the campaign toward the question of leadership. . . .

Wirthlin had described a clear strategy for handling the media in the campaign: create the themes, get them out in formats and environments that can be controlled, and minimize those situations in which the media can introduce events and issues that do not fit in with the campaign's themes. Part of the successful strategy is anticipating damaging situations that might develop that are out of the candidate's control and then sending out messages before the fact designed to minimize the impact.

It appeared that the candidate's capacity for manipulating the media in this way is a problem for the press. But, as Clymer pointed out, people do not seem to care that the candidate is not accessible, even though the media does, and both the candidates and the public express resentment at journalists aggressively intruding themselves into the campaign process in order to break the candidate's control over the flow of information.

Lewis noted that the one time in the 1980 campaign that the Reagan team momentarily lost control of the flow of information to the media was the occasion of former President Gerald Ford's vice-presidential "candidacy" during the Republican National Convention. The role of the networks in that piece of political history was the next subject for consideration.

The Dream Ticket

Wirthlin characterized the episode involving the negotiations with Ford and the reporting about it on television as the event over which the Reagan team had least control with respect to the media and also as the "least understood" major incident of the 1980 campaign.

From Wirthlin's perspective, the greatest confusion was over timing and communication:

> It was a case where there was nothing to see; the unseeing eye or the seeing eye of television went blind. The press accounts, the written accounts, were more accurate, but the point is this: The pre-discussions, the process that took place in about a thirty-six-hour period, were much more structured.

> Both the Ford camp and the Reagan camp were very much aware of what the parameters of that discussion were, and when it was evident that the circumstances and the nature of that offer were not acceptable in the form in which they were presented, there was absolutely no question in our mind, those of us who were on the Reagan side, that the Ford deal would never be put together.

For the Reagan camp, the offer itself to Ford had accomplished all that Wirthlin said they had wanted to do: "to unify and bring together the disparate elements of the Republican Party." The offer of the vice-presidency, independent of the acceptance of it, was enough both to avoid coming out of the convention with a liberal-conservative split and to bring Ford in as an effective political ally for the rest of the campaign.

According to Wirthlin, then, the Reagan team had for all practical purposes rejected the conditions before Ford went on television and discussed them. However, Ford had not yet been told that his terms were unacceptable. It was a case, John Deardourff said, of "an enormous number of reporters unable to find out enough and therefore speculating fairly widely and wildly about what was going on." Tom Brokaw noted that even leading Republican officials on the convention floor thought the deal had been consummated.

The conversation then turned to the networks' role in this affair and, in particular, to the live interview with Ford conducted by Walter Cronkite on CBS. Under questioning by Cronkite, Ford discussed the vice-presidential offer and some of the circumstances and conditions under which he might accept. The interview was seen and discussed by the rest of the media and by the convention delegates, and it created an enormous flurry of activity and expectation.

William Leonard, who was president of CBS News at the time, called the interview a "high point" of their coverage: "The fact that Walter . . . was able to fashion an interview that may or may not have been what President Ford had in mind when he sat down does not reflect badly on Walter as a journalist; quite the reverse." Martin Plissner also rose to Cronkite's defense:

> I don't think Walter has been given enough credit for what he did there. Ford came in there prepared to say and did say . . . that he told Reagan six weeks earlier that he wasn't interested and that was his position today. Within five minutes he has Betty Ford talking about how she would re-decorate the Vice President's mansion. . . . Ford is displaying an endless mastery of all the technicalities of a ticket with two candidates from the same state. . . . If this isn't enterprising journalism, I don't know what business we're in.

Leonard acknowledged that the fact that the interview was live may have "confused people and may have confused Jerry Ford, and may have confused everybody at the convention," but that did not make it improper.

Brokaw then picked up the story, recounting what then happened on the convention floor:

> My problem came later when a lot of people jumped from that interview to the fact that the ticket had been formed and the agreement struck. That's where things went afoul.

One of his producers told Brokaw to find Ford after the interview with Barbara Walters, which had followed the one with Cronkite. Brokaw caught up with Ford just off the convention floor. Here is his account of what happened next:

> I said, "Mr. President, you have got this place abuzz that you have made this deal," and he said, "You don't want to believe all the stuff you hear."

I said, "Well, what do you think are the chances?" He said, "The chances of this thing going through are extremely remote. I don't think we are going to be able to put this together. Betty is not crazy about moving back to Washington."

It was the damnedest thing you ever heard in your life: the difference between what he had said to Walter up there and the impact that that had, and what he said to me. I don't think he was trying to mislead either one of us. I think he was saying, "This is what you could do, Walter, if you work it out," . . . and he was saying to me, . . . "You know, this is not going to quite get together."

And that's what happened.

Roger Mudd recalled that he was home, watching the convention on television, and it looked to him as if CBS "did in fact put the ticket together, and that the network news division had a vested interest in that story because that story was developed by its two leading reporters. It took a very brave soul on the CBS news staff," he continued, "to go counter to the prevailing view, and nobody did, and that's why they got to where they got."

Where they got was that the networks, through the live interviews with Ford, had created a reality that missed one central fact—that Reagan's camp had already decided against the deal. But for a period of time it became the reality on which most of the delegates and Republican leaders relied and acted on. From the networks' point of view, they were quite appropriately talking to a central figure in a hot story. Retrospectively, it seems clear that the impression that was being created by braodcasting their interviews at the time they took place was an erroneous one that would have been corrected if they had asked the Reagan camp about the story. From the networks' perspective, it was "live" and there was no time to check out the story; from their point of view, there was even no need to because "the story" was happening right before their eyes and the eyes of the Republican leaders at the convention and millions of voters watching at home.

The discussion forced attention to the problems in live coverage of fast-breaking political stories, and the conference participants turned next to that issue.

Chasing the Fast-Breaking Story

Harold Bruno focused the problem:

Television and radio are reporting minute by minute; they don't have the luxury of having a few hours to the next edition. . . .

What happened in that case, from the standpoint of the reporters, was, you were getting what turned out to be good guidance from savvy political sources, but that was being countermanded by a fever that was sweeping the floor that the floor reporters, quite accurately, were reflecting. My recollection of it is our anchors constantly were using phrases such as, "This is what we are being told, but by no means is this certain." . . .

Bruce Morton said that he was luckily "running into people who said, 'No, it is not fixed; the ticket does not exist. It may, but it doesn't.' We had that on the air, too. It was who you bumped into, and you could hear a lot of different currents. That's the problem with doing this stuff live."

Precisely. And Clymer emphasized the point:

I was running around, getting the same crazy mixture of expectations and cold water that everybody else there was. I also had odd bits of time to watch television, and we had a couple of people sitting in the office watching as much as they could. I had a distinct sense that the television was very, very confusing, as the situation was for a reporter.

It was as though it was television of a live account of what was going on at any newsroom when some exciting story is breaking and I didn't have the sense (I don't quite know how you would do it) that there was somebody running any network program that said, "Hey, look, we are confusing the hell out of people; is there some way we can slow down?"

As Lewis then pointed out, it was a breaking story under highly competitive circumstances. Leonard explained:

We have been in several situations, all of us, lately, when we have been covering a story live, a very important story, assassinations among others. . . .

All of the warts and difficulties do show. In an ideal world, it would be nice if the executive producer or someone could say, "Hold it a second, fellows, let's wait, let's go into the other room and when we're absolutely sure who shot the Pope or whether the Presidential Press Secretary is alive or dead, then we will put it on; but until then, no information. Somehow, none of us are quite able to do that. . . .

Clymer suggested that such discretion seemed to have been exercised at the time of the Sadat assassination. But Brokaw pointed out that in that case the news flow was tightly controlled by the Egyptians, and the networks had no information to report.

It was Richard Wald who summed up the networks' perspective on covering fast-breaking stories in general and the "dream ticket" in particular. He returned to one of the themes from the Friday night session, namely, that this is one of the problems built in to the way that television is organized and that viewers use the medium:

I thought it was done reasonably well by television. The interesting thing to me was that this thing was happening in front of your eyes. . . . But at no

> time, at least on the network I was involved with, did we say that a deal had been made. . . .
>
> But one of the interesting things that happens in the course of that is nobody watches everything continuously. Especially if you were switching back and forth between the networks, all you had to do was miss a piece of that, and you could misinterpret what you saw at the instant it was on the air.
>
> The difference is, you can't roll the tape back a little bit with your hand and see what somebody just said five seconds ago. . . .

The problem is real. In an interview following the conference, Wirthlin said that Ford's going on television and discussing the terms and the negotiations came as a "complete absolute surprise" to the Reagan people and "raised a question" whether a deal could have been put together on any mutually acceptable basis. Thus it appears not only that the terms presented by Ford on live television had already been rejected, but that the interview itself had the effect of convincing the Reagan camp that there was no further purpose in talking with Ford about a possible ticket. When the Reagan people realized that the Ford interviews had generated momentum behind the ticket, to the point where some delegates thought the deal had been made, they were forced to move more quickly than they had intended to in offering the vice-presidential nomination to George Bush. That was the only way to put the nonstory of the dream ticket permanently to rest before Reagan, too, would have had to accept it as real. The intensity of television had created its own world, leaving the sense in the viewer that she knows the whole story because she has seen it with her own eyes.

Midterm Maneuvers

As a way of inviting the media managers to explore their perspectives and their concerns, Lewis asked them to consider the problem faced by a potential challenger to a popular president at the midpoint in his term at a time of high unemployment and a lingering recession.

David Garth suggested that the politicians were watching the president on television too much and admiring his performance more than the population at large was doing. He said that he would advise a potential candidate to attack the president on the issues, not personally.

Lewis asked him whether the candidate should have an alternative program before he starts criticizing the incumbent. Garth answered that the media would not be interested in a new program until the criticism had come:

> My experience has been that they, the reporters, do not want to hear your new ideas before you tear down the policies that are not working. . . .

I think that if you had a leading contender for the Democratic nomination, you could go first to the morning shows, some interview shows, the Sunday shows, and start to have that person verbalize an economic attack. Maybe have a major speech first and then do follow-ups. I think the networks and the newspapers would cover somebody who is attacking him. . . .

Gary Orren said that the polls indicated that people believe President Reagan's program is helping the rich and hurting the poor and that the economy is in trouble, but they do not seem to care too much about the former and assume that the economy will get better. Therefore, Orren continued, the theme he would try to develop is that "the President's program is hurting middle class Americans, taking away the American dream. . . ." Orren's view was that the "adversarial quality" of the press would make it very receptive to "a hard-hitting, substantive, issue-oriented attack."

David Gergen commented that because of the media, he would suggest a different strategy for a Democratic challenger:

I don't think I would advise them to go on a hard-hitting attack at this time; I think I would advise them to lay back and let the media do that for them. That . . . is occurring now, . . . and it is likely to continue until we see some kind of recovery.

What point is it for the Democrats now to make that into a partisan issue? I think they are better off to establish the legitimacy of the points they want to make through others. . . .

Garth disagreed:

What's happening now is that the press is really carrying the battle. . . . It is time for someone who wants to run for president to stand up now and start to enunciate those things.

The problem you have as a Democrat . . . is . . . when you go through the candidates, candidate by candidate, the same thing comes through: not enough appeal, not enough strength, not enough image, not enough guts. . . .

In order for someone to start to develop, you are going to have to take strong positions. I would suggest the economic issue is one thing, and I would not be afraid of a comeback that we are tearing down the house.

Ronald Brown stated it even more strongly:

I don't think we can wait for the press to do it for us. I think there are some things that the press can do and some things it can't.

The press can talk about policies, they can show unemployment data, they can talk about rising inflation; but unless you can tie that to Ronald Reagan, from a Democratic point of view, you can't win.

It is true that the president has been able to separate himself from those policies in the minds of most Americans, and now is the time to make most Americans think it is his fault, that he is responsible for those policies.

George Reedy questioned whether a politician's attack on Reagan would be more effective than the press attack:

The press is saying that he is responsible or rather his policies are responsible for the collapse of the housing market. Mr. MacNeil almost every other night on his program has somebody that comes up and explains that we have got a lot of unemployment and this is all because of Mr. Reagan and all because of the Japanese and various other things. . . .

If the public is not going to take attacks seriously coming from the press, which theoretically is not trying to get into the White House, why should an attack by a politician, who obviously is looking for a job, make an impact?

Garth responded that the press attacks were already having an effect on Reagan's popularity, and it would have been far greater if it were not for the sympathy from the press and the public after the assassination attempt. Garth reiterated his earlier point: Even if the press's message is getting through, someone who wants to run for president has to "get out in front. You can't let the press do the fighting for you."

Christopher Arterton suggested that for Democrats who wanted to carve out a leadership role, local television might be more fertile territory for visibility than network television since it is at the local level that the budget cuts are directly felt.

Richard E. Neustadt commented on the lack of alternative policies being resented by Democrats and agreed that the reason the Democrats were not coming up with "solutions" is that the heart of viable alternatives is income policy. The politicians are "terrified even to mention the term, much less to develop a viable scheme." Clymer seemed to agree, observing that the Democrats who want to run for president are attacking all right but that "because they are not doing it with singular panache, and they are not doing it with singularly interesting solutions, they don't seem to be quite as newsworthy. They get covered a bit, but they don't get covered a whole lot." Finally, Congressman Obey added that the presidential candidates had to come up with solutions; if they do not, "the people will be saying what the networks are saying, on nightly news, which is that the Democrats really haven't presented any other alternatives."

Lewis asked R. Brown whether he thought that the president's apparent capacity to separate himself personally from the impacts of his own policies was the fault of the press. Brown's response went beyond Lewis's inquiry to the heart of the relationship between the networks and the politicians. He suggested that the tensions exist and are inevitable but that improvements could be made:

The greatest animosity is probably felt within a family, and when you are out on the campaign trail, you become a family; that is, the people who are out there with the candidate and the people in the media.

It has to happen. You are sharing the same lousy hotels and lousy meals and lousy buses. You empathize with each other, and you get very offended when someone in the media who is your friend and who you have been living with all these months says something that you think is unfair to your candidate. . . .

Occasionally, there is a tendency on the part of the people in the media to . . . make sure that they are not taken in, that these relationships do not allow them to remain objective. But I think that is the nature of the beast. That's a human response that I almost think we have to live with.

I hope that as we identify these problems, not that they are clear answers, [that we can also identify] some clear modifications that can be made in what we do.

It was an ideal bridge to the discussion of concerns of the politicians about network coverage.

The Candidates' Complaints

John Deardourff summarized the issues that were of particular importance to the politicians with regard to policy and practice of the media in covering the presidential elections:

I would hope that in the future, as has happened occasionally in the past, we would have somewhat more ease of access to paid time with flexible time segments.

I would personally like to see more emphasis by the news programs on straight comparisons of the views of the candidates on the major issues. . . .

It would be helpful to have a little discussion on the subject of the extent to which the television and radio, and to some extent newspapers as well, and the magazines, make news or report their own news. One of the things that has been kind of fascinating me is the way in which polling has become a story of its own. I mean, they pay for the polls, they take the polls, they report them on their news programs as news. There is nothing wrong with that, but then you get into the question of selectivity; and the decisions they make to use polling or to do it at all affects and in some cases, it seems to me, distorts the political process.

As an example, Deardourff cited the instance of the networks going to Florida in 1979 and polling delegates at the state party conventions. To him, that was a clear case in which the networks distorted the importance of the event. "Why was that viewed as so significant," he asked, "that they had to spend that kind of money, polling people whose vote wasn't going to matter anyway?"

The network participants defended their activity in Florida. Mitofsky pointed out that Senator Edward Kennedy and President Carter had spent "several hundred thousand dollars campaigning" in anticipation of the state convention. And Plissner added that the Florida Democratic State Committee thought the straw poll was important and official enough to count the votes.

It was something of a chicken-or-egg issue again. As Deardourff asked, "Did we spend money because you were doing the polling, or did you spend money because we were . . . ?" Bruno answered by suggesting that this was "the classic example of two state political parties manipulating us. If there ever was a story that all of us did not want to cover, it was the contrived straw vote that first of all the Florida Democrats and later on the Florida Republicans were going to stage in the fall, in October of 1979."

As Bruno recalled the situation, despite the reluctance on the part of the networks to give much attention to the Florida straw polls, Carter decided "to show some political muscle and make a contest out of it." The networks then decided to revise their plans and go to Florida, but at the same time they also decided to "carefully explain to people that this is a meaningless straw vote, but it is a test of whether or not the White House—and at the time Jimmy Carter was in considerable political trouble—can get itself together."

The next issue for the networks was whether to do their own polling. They decided to do selective polling themselves, according to Bruno, because they could not get results from areas outside of Dade County fast enough for their Saturday night newscasts. Bruno and Plissner distinguished what happened in Florida from the networks' doing their own poll: The preferences were being tabulated by the state committees, and the networks were just trying to get the results faster than the committees could provide them. Under questioning by Deardourff and Clymer, Plissner acknowledged that CBS did poll all the delegates at the Republican convention.

The real question in all of this discussion was not whether the networks followed the politicians or vice versa but whether the network coverage, however explained, gave the events in Florida significance disproportionate to what those proceedings ought to have had. Garth thought the answer was yes:

> The television coverage by definition is not meaningless. Even if they say it is meaningless, the fact that they are there and it is on the air makes it important. That's, I think, one of the problems that John [Deardourff] has with something like a non-event that becomes an event with television coverage, even though it says it is meaningless.

Are the Solutions Worse Than the Problems?

Gergen recounted his own list of complaints: the emphasis on the horse-race aspects of the campaign, the very small segments devoted to issues, and the sarcasm that comes at the end of stories. He then turned the focus of the discussion to the two "solutions" offered earlier by Richard Salant, namely, going from a half-hour to an hour for daily network news and repealing Section 315 of the communications act, the equal-time/equal-opportunity law:

> I'm very interested in knowing, first of all, how television is going to use that extra half an hour. I think it is one of the most important questions facing us in terms of campaign coverage in 1984. And secondly, if we do get rid of 315, how are we going to use that?

In response to a question from Lewis, among the participants only Mudd, Clymer, and Dot Ridings indicated that they would favor keeping Section 315. Clymer said that his concern was not with the networks but with local outlets and "how they would behave toward favorite candidates" if they were free of 315.

Lewis then turned the conversation to Gergen's first point, the networks' ideas about the use of the extra half-hour of daily news. Leonard, the first to comment, connected the two issues:

> Certainly and clearly, in campaign years, if we had an hour of evening news, a lot of the problems that we now face because of 315 would disappear. Clearly a great deal of the hour during a political campaign would be devoted to political news, and it would become very, very difficult to persuade our masters at the network to give us any appreciable additional time, even if it were not barred for other reasons; that would be considered enough. . . .
>
> Obviously, there would be longer pieces. Obviously there would be more pieces. Obviously, there would be broader coverage. Obviously, there would be more coverage in general.
>
> I think we all probably have somewhat different ideas. I personally envision a broadcast that would have in it every night something of substance in terms of length, and . . . a diversity of commentary, opinion, that there simply isn't enough time for now.

Jeffrey Gralnick offered his views:

> I think the fairest criticism of the half-hour broadcast is that it is insufficient to the task of covering the news day in and day out. . . .

Unquestionably, the first thing we will do with the extra time is make the reporting more complete and make the reporting less superficial. Specifically, if you were planning the 1984 campaign now and want to know, if we have an hour broadcast by 1984 will your problem of reaching the public with your explanation of the issues be solved, I can't answer that honestly.

Arterton asked Stuart Loory, who already has a lot more time than the networks do for campaign coverage, what Cable News Network's (CNN) plans are for 1984. Loory said CNN would probably do some things very much like the networks and some things differently. Like the other networks, they would assign reporters to campaigns and then rotate them after a considerable period of time. Then he talked about what they will do differently and suggested some of his own concerns about problems of coverage:

What we do differently is give much more time to our stories, considerably more, so that we have time to do a more complete job of reporting what the candidates are saying about the various issues. We will not . . . expend the amount of time and the amount of effort sending our anchor people to the key primary states to anchor our shows from there. . . . We can devote more of our efforts to doing the coverage of the candidates, [and] also into doing the coverage of the states and what impact the candidates are making in the primary states.

One of the things that concerns me about what all of us are doing at the present time is that we are very event oriented, that the amount of effort, by the networks, going into election coverage is going into such things as constructing fancy sets in various cities around the country to report results and to report the horse race.

We seem to think we are discharging our obligation to cover the election by covering those particular events along with the convention. So that the big numbers during the election year are the coverage from primary states, coverage of the election, and the grand finale, which is the election night coverage.

In the electronic news business, one of the things we miss that print is still doing better is the coverage of the candidates and what they are saying. I sometimes get the feeling that our coverage is more the coverage of the people, the voters, rather than the candidates. . . . We're giving the candidates a free ride.

Are the politicians concerned that if the extra half-hour of news is devoted to increased coverage of issues, that the networks would be setting the political agenda? Gergen said no; he expects that twice as much time for news will mean twice as much of what is offered now and will increase the tedium: "If we have twice as much of the same hoopla over the course of the campaign, I think we will be exhausted by September."

Brokaw wondered about what the politicians' plans were for taking advantage of that extra half-hour of news. He recounted his experience during the closing days of the 1980 campaign when political operatives would call the network, "offering" one or another leading politician for his morning interview.

Mudd then picked up the conversation and suggested another problem, from his perspective, with the way the networks were covering campaigns:

> One of the things that has happened to nightly news reporting in the last four or five years is that pieces, correspondents' pieces, have gotten shorter. I think all of us remember doing two and a half and three minute pieces. . . . Now, generally, they are like one minute twenty or one minute thirty. . . . As the competition has increased, the pace has had to quicken. . . .
>
> Things have to pop and crackle.

Deardourff questioned Mudd about who decides how long each piece will be. Mudd answered that "there are executive producers and assistant producers, and they sort of hand out the times." Mudd described the process of a producer in the field calling in to report what he has, and the producers allocating time to that piece based on what their other commitments happen to be.

Deardourff wondered whether there was research of some kind supporting the trend toward shorter pieces. Mudd answered that he did not know of any; it was more in the nature of the way the business was organized:

> I think it is the natural tendency of a broadcast that it wants to cover as much ground as it can, to cover ground quickly and in a brisk, vigorous kind of way. I see no reason to believe that if we get a sixty-minute broadcast that the pieces necessarily will be any longer. If we are trying to compete for someone's attention, and we have decided that their attention won't last more than a minute-thirty with a thirty-minute broadcast, why would it last five minutes on an hour broadcast?

Morton and Wald pointed out that some longer pieces do run now, even in the thirty-minute broadcast. Mudd said that his network did about three a week. Morton suggested that an hour would give them the opportunity to do more longer pieces. Mudd responded by suggesting that the thirty-minute broadcast was impossible and the hour news would not be inherently much better:

> What you are limited to now on a thirty-minute broadcast, with the spot breaking story, covering the candidate in the field, is pretty much black and white. There is not time for gray. On an hour broadcast you would get some time for gray, but not really much. I do not think that an hour broadcast is going to solve the great problems we all have; . . . we will still have the same problem.

Deardourff pointed out the parallel between the politicians' views of effective advertising and the networks' views of effective programming:

> I keep hearing these criticisms of the thirty-second or sixty-second commercial as though there is something horrible about that; and at the same time I'm now hearing that somebody has decided that a minute-twenty is all that the public can absorb. I mean, that's why we're doing it our way, just as that's why they're doing it their way.

Frank Reynolds was more optimistic:

> I'm inclined to agree with Roger that we're not going to solve all our problems by simply getting an hour. But I would also point out that . . . television news right now is a question of seconds. And sometimes, if we can just lengthen . . . those individual spots by, let's say, a negligible twenty seconds . . .

William Small suggested another theory to explain why the length of the typical piece had shrunk to a minute-twenty, and he then offered another view of what would happen with an hour-long news broadcast:

> What has happened . . . is the technology has made it so much easier for us, so much more expensive as well, but so much easier for us to get material, that now the political reporting and all reporting is competing with far more material than was ever available to us in the past. And that continues to grow. Something happens in Italy, and there is a flood of material almost instantly available, certainly by nightfall here. That would not have been true some time ago.

> But I would like to speak to the question of what would happen in an hour in terms of a political campaign. Right now, we cover, it seems to me, four aspects of politics. The one that is of greatest interest and has had the most attention is the horserace. Secondly, we try to cover the nature of the candidates, who they are and what they are, and in time that becomes less important, because your public begins to know and other things take over.

> Thirdly, we deal with the issues. All three networks, in the last campaign and in earlier campaigns, have made an attempt to define where the candidates stand on the issues, sometimes with their cooperation and sometimes with our own research because they really want to limit the number of issues. In many ways, when I hear a political figure saying, "you never report the issues," what he is really saying is, "you have embarrassed my candidate with some report and I wish the hell you would talk about those serious issues that interest us more.

> And lastly, we cover what I've always called "There goes the balloon," which is what you guys [the political consultants] do for a living; and that has increased in every campaign I have witnessed in my lifetime. We now do it with regularity on all three networks. We talk about the media manipulators, how they do it, what they are doing. Some of the cynicism and some of the smart-ass stuff that people complain about really is in that kind of a piece, and deservedly so.

When Tom Pettit or Bruce Morton or somebody goes behind the scenes and shows how they released the doves at the right moment and the balloons went and all the rest of it, sure, it makes them look a little bit silly and we cynical, and I think properly so. . . .

We find these four elements competing for time, and they can't all get on right now. When we do a series on the issues, we have to take time away from something else. With an hour, you not only can do both, but we can do something that we rarely do now. We treat the issues in terms of where the candidates stand and what he or she has said, but we don't have enough time to say how others view those issues: how do the labor unions and the AMA and the party workers and the man on the street, how do they deal with that?

Small also added that in a presidential election year, more stories about campaigns for governor and for the House and Senate would be aired in an hour nightly news program. Congressman Obey was not pleased:

Listening to what Mr. Small has just said does not reassure me very much, because what I think I hear is that there are a lot more things going to be packed into that hour.

I do not want to see national television involved in more congressional races. I don't want to see them going out and asking what the labor unions and this and that group think about the issues, because I don't think that television has the capacity, whether it is a half hour or an hour, to deal with these issues in anything other than a black and white way.

I'm very skeptical that we will in the end create a greater understanding of the public of these issues. What I really wish you would do if you had more time is not give any of it to the candidates. I wish you would do what Tom Brokaw was talking about, to use that time to get more into what the issues are that the country confronts without relationship to what the candidates are saying about those issues. I think you have a far greater capacity to deal with that than you do with the positions of the candidates on the issues.

The other point I would like to make is that I think the more time television will have to deal with campaigns, the more jaded it will leave the public. . . . No matter how much time you have available, it will still simplify the issues, because that is the nature of the medium, in my judgment. And when politicians cannot measure up to those issues by being able to deal with them in a simplified way, then we get left holding the bag. . . .

And I would certainly hope, that there would be less, not more coverage of the early primaries, because, to the extent that you have greater time available to candidates in those early primaries, you are going to make those primaries even more important and make it less likely that the parties have an opportunity to adjust to changing events by selecting candidates at a later time, regardless of what the Democratic rules are going to be.

As the session drew to a close, some of the political consultants commented on their role in the campaigns. Lewis described the current presidential selection process as a system in which "choices are made by an interplay between a small group of political managers and the press, primarily television."

Wirthlin was the first to respond:

> I think it would be not completely candid if we said we didn't have doubts concerning our role in the process. I think most of us recognize that in some cases that role can be pivotal. . . .

> There must be something beyond simply electing someone to an office. There has to be a personal investment in that candidate to make that relationship what it should be.

Lewis narrowed the issue, asking Deardourff whether he was concerned that the current system, dominated by the managers and the media, was an inadequate replacement for the political parties? Deardourff was not bothered at all:

> I think that the technological change that has taken place in both the media and in travel and in a variety of other ways has led almost inevitably to the creation of this little mini-industry, and I don't feel the least bit uncomfortable in terms of the role we play, or in general the level of both qualitative excellence and ethical conduct we bring to all of this.

> If you begin with the premise that political activity, political campaigns, are really the business of a free country, a free society, and that the electoral process itself is the only way we select our leaders, and that what we are attempting is to present the best case we can for the election of people for whom we work, and that we do think long and hard about for whom we do that (obviously you have disappointments), . . . I don't have any regrets about the role we play or about the way in which we play it.

Garth suggested that the system is a lot better than it used to be:

> What bothers me is the so-called good old days. Who are these people who ran campaigns before? . . . They were much more hidden than we are.

> I think the press has access to us, and they hit us plenty of times, and I think they should. But I'm not sure in the old days, when three guys in Chicago went into the back room with Carmine DeSapio and someone else from New York, that the process was helped, or that the issues the candidate was forced to run on were the candidate's issues, or the issues of that particular interest group.

> I think most of us in the business today do not try to attempt to change the positions of candidates, especially where they have had exposure for six years in the Senate or they have been a governor somewhere. You really can't do it. In the old days,when you bought the party, you bought the party line right down.

Rafshoon agreed:

> You may have doubts, but . . . I feel a lot more comfortable with utilizing
> the mass media to present your case than the good old days when somebody
> in the South and somebody in New York and a bunch of newspaper editors
> around the country could endorse somebody and that was the choice given
> to the people. I think I would rather see it presented through the mass
> media than the back rooms.

Afterword

The bias of the politicians and their managers was clear at this session: they
are interested in maximizing control over the flow of information during
the campaign, particularly the message that they themselves are putting
out. A good campaign strategy is one in which the messages are planned
and plotted, timed to build on one another as the campaign progresses. In
1980 both Reagan and Carter adopted strategies that minimized the opportunity for live interviews and unplanned inquiries that might have changed
the focus, interrupted the flow, or introduced new elements into the campaign. Quite rightly, the media feel manipulated by such orchestration,
and they therefore try to disrupt the messages with their own questions,
sometimes by pointing out to their viewers just how the communication is
being controlled. They acknowledge, however, that the public does not
seem much interested in their concerns.

The dream-ticket episode was the one time in the 1980 campaign
when the Reagan effort almost lost control. It is a particularly relevant
case for this discussion because the disruption was initiated by the networks, not by Reagan's political opponents. From the networks' point
of view, they were performing well, covering and advancing a hot story.
From the Reagan perspective, they were making news, not reporting
it. Retrospectively, it appears that by acceding to the competitive and
institutional pressures to pursue a breaking story on live television, what
they were showing viewers was in essence a piece of the news-gathering
process, not a finished product that would meet the journalistic standards for a piece on the nightly news. Is the pressure to do that over-
whelming? Or should we be able to expect some restraint? In this case,
had any of the networks sought out and received timely comment from a
Reagan spokesperson on the state of the Ford deal, it is likely that
there would have been no misleading impression conveyed; the Ford interview would have gone down in history as an interesting footnote about
what might have been, not a television event that forced the hand of the
Republican nominee. Covering fast-breaking stories with no deadlines is

tricky enough; live coverage dramatically increases the risk of conveying something other than the whole truth and creating a new, media-made reality.

The next issue of media intrusion concerned the source of critical commentary about an administration during the middle of its term, before the reelection campaign has formally begun. There seemed to be a shared view that in the current situation the media was bearing the responsibility for being the loyal opposition and that the coverage was having an effect on Reagan's popularity. The politicos agreed that the media were also beginning to point out that the political opposition was providing no alternatives and also that potential Democratic candidates for president would have to begin to carve out positive and individualized images for themselves if they wanted to be taken seriously for the fight in 1984.

The complaints about the networks' coverage of Reagan and his programs depended to some extent on whether you were on Reagan's side or not, but the politicians did move on to more generalized criticisms of the networks' role in the presidential campaign. Again, what the consultants wanted was more availability of better time for advertisements, coverage of the issues the candidates were addressing, and reflection in coverage of the relative importance the candidates' placed on particular events and stops along the road to the nomination and election.

This perspective was evident during the discussion on what would happen with the extra time available if the networks went to an hour-long daily news program. Most of the network people saw hope for fuller coverage. The politicians were not overly optimistic, expecting that the pressures and constraints of the business would force the networks to use the second half-hour for more of the same. The network claimed they would provide longer individual pieces, more coverage of the issues, more national coverage of state campaigns, and more opportunity to present problems in their full complexity.

The political consultants were hardly forced into the kind of hard self-analysis that their network counterparts had undertaken earlier in the afternoon. But their point of view was clear: One of their goals was to control the message. They see the democratic process served by the media enabling the candidates to say what to say when they want to say it, and they have great skepticism about the media's claim of just reporting events rather than participating in them. They have very little confidence that any reforms will overcome the institutional and competitive pressures to perform as the networks have in the past.

6

Government, Networks, or Politicians: Who Should Produce the Presidential Election Show?

Major Dramatis Personae (in Order of Appearance)

William Small, President, NBC News

Tyrone Brown, Moderator, former Commissioner, Federal Communications Commission; Member, Steptoe & Johnson

William Leonard, President, CBS News

Ben H. Bagdikian, Professor, Graduate School of Journalism, University of California at Berkeley

Richard Wald, Senior Vice-President, ABC News

Adam Clymer, Political Correspondent, *New York Times*

Irwin Segelstein, Vice-Chairman of the Board, NBC Inc.

Ronald H. Brown, Deputy Chairman, Democratic National Committee, Partner, Patton, Boggs & Blow

Stephen A. Sharp, General Counsel, Federal Communications Commission

Henry Geller, Director, Washington Center for Public Policy Research

Gary Orren, Associate Professor of Public Policy, John F. Kennedy School of Government

Roger Mudd, Chief Washington Correspondent, NBC News

Dot Ridings, First Vice-President and Communications Chair, League of Women Voters of the United States

The mission for the Sunday morning session was to explore the laws and regulations that affect presidential election coverage, to ask whether they serve the public interest in an open and robust political process, and to speculate on the effect of various suggestions for amendment or repeal. The focus was on two provisions of the communications act: Section 312(a)(7), known as "reasonable access," and Section 315(a), known as "equal opportunity" or "equal time."

Section 312(a)(7) says that the Federal Communications Commission may revoke any station license "for willful or repeated failure to allow reasonable access to or to permit purchase of reasonable amounts of time for the use of a broadcasting station by a legally qualified candidate for Federal elective office on behalf of his candidacy."

Section 315(a) requires that "if any licensee shall permit any person who is a legally qualified candidate for any public office to use a broadcasting station, he shall afford equal opportunities to all other such candidates in the use of such station. . . ."

The Regulatory Rationale

Early in the session, during the discussion of the reasonable-access law, William Small made the point that the law intrudes on the discretion of the television programmer to a substantial degree and

> had either the courts or a government agency intruded on a newpaper's decision, we would all say it is outrageous and unconstitutional. My point is that because it is television, a regulated industry, quite cavalierly no one raised that question.

His comments triggered a discussion about the original argument for regulating television and whether the reasoning still applied and still justified the scheme of laws and regulations under which the television industry now operates.

Moderator Tyrone Brown, a former commissioner of the Federal Communications Commission, suggested that government moves in where it feels pressure to do so and that there has been no intrusion into newspapers because "that kind of pressure" is not felt with respect to newspapers. William Leonard said that there was a commercial reason why such pressures did not exist:

> Few if any newspapers are, by any reasonable definition, mass media, and the pressure doesn't exist because the circulation, the reach, and the implication of power doesn't exist. . . .

T. Brown wondered whether the distinction between print and electronic, the explanation for why there was enough pressure to regulate one and not the other, had something to do with the fact that the television news executive must fit the news into the available time slot whereas the print news executive has the capacity to expand to shrink the "news hole" to accommodate the quantity of information he wants to report. Leonard acknowledged that the pressures were different in that regard, but said he doubted whether that difference was enough to justify regulation.

Ben Bagdikian mentioned another kind of pressure:

> If a politician asks for a full-page ad in a newspaper and is denied it, he or she, the politician, can invent their own somewhat comparable medium in a big mass mailing, and they do. But on broadcasting, the local stations have a government, criminally enforced monopoly on a frequency, and the politician can't reinvent that.

Essentially, Bagdikian was relying on the idea of scarcity of airways to justify regulation, the principal notion used when the Supreme Court upheld the constitutionality of the communications act and the FCC regulations. Leonard dismissed it as anachronistic:

> There are two newspapers in New York. There are seventy-seven radio stations. There are seven television stations. There are thirty-six cable channels. That argument is going out of style. . . .

Small added that

> as a practical matter, anyone can put together a network by buying local time. It is done all the time in sports. Billy Graham does it. All kinds of people do it. If you are denied or don't want to go to a network, there are a lot of ad agencies who will buy you time in every city in the country and create a network for you.

Bagdikian protested that even so, "if the stations deny it, there is nothing the applicant can do to get on the air." Richard Wald began to draw out the distinction between newspapers and broadcast, suggesting that when it is examined fairly, it does not hold. He used as his example the one offered by Bagdikian, the request for purchasing time or space for a political advertisement. Wald pointed out that the candidate wants prime time on television, the network's best three hours of its available twenty-four hours. That is analogous, Wald continued, to the candidate insisting that the *Wall Street Journal* run his ad in its prime space, say the first seven pages. So Wald's first point is that the request for prime time on television has to be seen as comparable to a request for equally prime space in a newspaper, a request, he suggested, with which newspapers would often not comply. They would not comply because to sell a huge political ad in the first seven pages of the newspaper would disrupt the most important part of the paper's product, in the same way, he was suggesting, that selling a candidate five minutes or a half-hour of prime time on a network would disrupt the most important part of their product.

Wald's second point carried the hypothetical case into court. There, he hypothesized,

> The *Wall Street Journal* says "First Amendment, First Amendment, First Amendment." The court says, "Oh, I don't know. Here you are. You are distributed over the air. This thing goes from a composing room up in the air all over the country, scarce airways. No other newspaper in the country uses that process. It belongs to the people. *Wall Street Journal*, you're wrong. Print it in the first seven pages."

Wald's argument, of course, is that the distinction is getting more and more blurred. Sharp pointed out that the distinction will be even more difficult to maintain if newspapers are delivered electronically, into homes through cable. Wald said that Bagdikian was "positing a system that used to work, but the system is in the process of change."

Adam Clymer argued that the newspapers' relationships to the political process had also changed:

> There used to be a lot of newspapers in most cities, and most newspapers used to be identifiable with political parties. . . . But as newspapers have shrunk, they are a great deal less partisan, and I think they are a great deal more willing to accept political advertisements in almost any time or season. . . . The suggestion that we go around making decisions that it is too early to sell an ad . . . is frivolous.

Wald responded to Clymer by reiterating his central point:

> What I am suggesting is that unexamined in the discussion over this problem is the fact that the regulation (aside from the fact that most regulation springs from power: you can do it, therefore you do do it) is based on a view of technology that is becoming outmoded. . . . Newspapers are getting fewer. Multiplication of electronic technologies is making them wider. There are more radio stations. There are going to be drop-in television stations. There is more cable. . . .
>
> The logical foundation for some of the regulation is changing, but the regulation isn't. . . . The logic that leads you to get to the legislative process or the regulatory process is breaking up.
>
> I'm not saying that Congress or the FCC doesn't have the power to do it. I'm saying that unexamined is the base upon which the power resides. . . . If newspapers do become, in essence, public utilities in geographically limited areas, [they] ought to be regulated and we ought not.

Who Should Decide When the Campaign Begins?

The first specific regulatory issue addressed was reasonable access. T. Brown began by asking the networks to explain what happened when the Carter/Mondale committee tried, in October 1979, to buy a half-hour of

prime time in early December to begin the reelection effort. The committee's request, which was refused by all three networks, eventually led to an
FCC decision and a court case. Irwin Segelstein was the only network
corporate executive, as distinguished from news executive, at the table, and
he responded to Brown.

Segelstein said the first consideration, discussed by the appropriate
network decision makers and lawyers, was "to find out what obligation we
had" under the current laws and FCC regulations. He pointed out that from
the network's point of view there were interests that wanted to keep the
schedule from being disrupted by selling a large block of prime time to a
political campaign:

> There is a public we serve with entertainment programs and a news sched-
> ule, and producers who make those programs who would like to see them
> on the air.

From that perspective, he continued, the question was, if the campaign were
to start then, would the schedule be disrupted without the lead time necessary to alter programs by shortening them? Would that be "too early" and
would it create "chaos" for NBC and its affiliates? T. Brown asked him
what he meant by "too soon to interrupt your normal program schedule"?
Segelstein answered that while the "public service obligation overtones
were there," it was basically "a business issue." It was not simply the
interruption, he said, but

> if the process interferes with the sampling and popularity of programs, not
> merely for the short term, but potentially leading to program failure over a
> long period of time. . . . There is a constituency within the network that
> likes the entertainment schedule to get a chance to work.

Leonard added that there was a concern at the networks that if the political
season, as far as paid television was concerned, began in December in the
last election, it would simply be moved back earlier and earlier. If it began in
September, he pointed out, that was the start of the entertainment schedule
season, which is

> the most difficult time in the scheduling of a network's schedule, the
> most difficult time from the point of view of the habits of the audience,
> the most difficult time from the competitive standpoint among the three
> networks. . . .

Segelstein noted that in 1979 the networks had been through a strike and
therefore the entertainment schedule was premiering at about the same time
as the request came from the Carter/Mondale committee:

> If you sit in this room and you believe that what we're talking about is of
> immense importance, you must also grant the point of view of people who

are not here, that the public is just as much concerned with entertainment programs. Frequently, the public is more concerned with seeing their favorite program than their favorite politician. . . .

Clymer recalled that the networks had already turned down requests from other candidates for similar blocks of time so they had reason to believe that if they sold the time, the requests would increase and begin earlier. Segelstein reinforced his case with two further points: First, he said that the Carter/Mondale committee request was for a half-hour, that NBC did not have more than two half-hours they could sell, and that those two half-hours were then carrying very successful programs, thereby producing a lot of revenue that was supporting the less lucrative time in the schedule. Then he argued that the proximate upcoming election was the Iowa primary and that candidates had other opportunities for getting their message across: local paid time and free time on regular local and national newscasts that were covering the Iowa contest.

In sum, the case for refusing the request for time rested on several points: the interests both within the network and in the public in not disturbing the entertainment schedule, particularly during premiere period or key ratings periods; the short-term and potential long-term revenue loss from such interruption; the likelihood that granting the request would lead to more requests made earlier in the season; and the availability of other outlets for the candidates. The case for not selling the time, and implicitly for allowing the networks to make the decision within their own discretion, having been made, Ronald Brown stated the position of the politicians:

> It seems to me a candidate ought to have the right to buy time when a candidate needs time; and although I am very much for a shorter campaign season, for a lot of reasons, it somewhat distresses me that networks can decide how long a campaign season is going to be (or at least play an important role in making that decision), and that one of the factors that might have gone into that decision (along with business factors, which are certainly legitimate), is what is the right length of time for a campaign season and when should it start. I'm not sure that is an appropriate matter for networks to make a determination on.

In response to a question about who should make that judgment, Brown continued:

> Well, it seems to me that the political parties have a very important stake in that judgment. And it seems to me the candidates have a very important stake in the judgment. And it seems to me that the public, through regulatory agencies that regulate the election process, have an important stake. . .

His comment about the public set off an exchange between himself, Wald, and Leonard about who ascertains what the public wants and whether any of the relevant interests would be guided by such a determination if it were made:

> Wald: Who interprets what the public's view is?
>
> R. Brown: Well, I think it depends on the issue. In some cases the Federal Communications Commission does that, and in some cases the Federal Elections Commission does that. In some cases the courts have had to do that.
>
> Wald: Do they interpret what the public's view is, or do they interpret what the legal implications are?
>
> R. Brown: Both.
>
> Wald: Is there another case of the political process in essence preempting the basic corporate structure of a private business?
>
> R. Brown: I don't understand the relevance of that question since it is already accepted that this industry is a different kind of business.
>
> Wald: I guess you are right.
>
> R. Brown: It requires a different kind of regulation.
>
> Leonard: Suppose there was some kind of clear and accepted evidence that the public's view was that: until a certain date, interruption of their regular service by political candidates of any kind, except in regularly scheduled news programs, was something that the public did not wish overwhelmingly? How would you regard that?
>
> R. Brown: I think it is a factor that you would consider.
>
> Wald: But you wouldn't be guided by it; in other words, the public's desire would not necessarily rule?
>
> R. Brown: I think it would be a factor. It wouldn't necessarily rule. I think there would be other factors.

At that point, Moderator T. Brown asked whether the networks were making their decisions on whether to sell time based on what they perceived to be the desires of the public? Segelstein answered that he thought it was reasonable to believe that "the public would prefer to see the regular programming" without a large number of interruptions. He noted that politicians understand the negative reaction of the public to disruption of the expected entertainment schedule:

> When we get requests from incumbent presidents for air time, they never ask for Monday night on ABC when the football game is on. They are quite aware of what sort of interruption would not only displease, but would enrage viewers.

Stephen Sharp raised two broader issues that had been suggested by the previous exchange. First was whether the networks should separate the issue of the public's interest from the networks' best financial interest:

The nature of networks and television in general is one of serving the public interest in a pecuniary sense; that is, if the public doesn't like what they see, the networks don't make much money, and some networks make more money than others. So, as a result, the competition is designed to fine-tune the network's sensitivity to what people want.

Now, the question of how do you determine what the public wants need not necessarily be separated from pecuniary interests; it can be but it doesn't have to be. . . . The networks obviously would prefer to have continuity of programming, and therefore you might think that is a rather crass motive, but nevertheless it reflects, in fact I think, what the public has in mind.

Having made his case that the networks are on solid ground ascertaining the public's interest by looking at what the public desires to watch, Sharp went on to consider another issue, namely, whether government agencies were appropriate bodies to make such determinations:

We were talking about the FEC and the FCC, and to the extent that we want to operate on the premise that broadcasting is accepted as a different type of business, that's fine; but I'm not sure I'm ready to accept the premise.

Henry Geller objected to the notion that television and the networks ought to be treated as just another business:

I would like to quarrel with that. I think this is a business impressed with the public interest. The public acts through Congress, and if Congress wants to adopt a statute (I think it is a bum statute that they adopted) . . . that says . . . that a politician should be given access to time when he requests it unless there are extraordinary circumstances, that is the public talking. We talk in this country through Congress. The only thing that stops that is the Constitution.

Sharp did not let the issue rest:

If we are going to say this type of business is different, the essential difference is that the government should be out of it, not in it, because it has serious First Amendment implications. . . . This type of regulation, reasonable access, whatever you want to call it, . . . where the government is injecting itself into the process of what people can see or hear, that type of regulation should be abolished.

For the politicians, the spirit of the First Amendment compels regulation of television, or at the very least legitimizes it; for Sharp and the networks the First Amendment prohibits such government involvement.

Elizabeth Drew raised a concern about the logical extension of the idea, embodied in R. Brown's position on access, that the politicians ought to be able to buy time whenever they want to do so:

What are we doing to the system itself; what premium are we then putting on wealth and the ability to raise extraordinary amounts of money?

Does that in itself become a distortion of the process, as opposed to the news coverage which does take upon itself to try to provide balance? Are you saying that the wealthiest candidate can just buy time as much as possible?

Clymer noted that in one respect what Drew foresees has already come to pass:

The Republican National Committee buys, at least from the perspective of the Democratic National Committee, a lot of time on television in thirty- and sixty-second spots. The Republican National Committee and the congressional and Senate committees, you know, can spend more money on that in a year than the three Democratic committees seem able to raise . . . in a year. So there is that degree of noncandidate distortion. . . . We have to a degree what Liz is talking about already.

Segelstein suggested that it might be better to wait and see what happens:

It may be that the desire to buy a lot of time may change when the returns are in from the first candidate who buys time and gets phone calls about the disruption. . . .

Small argued that there are principled reasons for turning down an early request to buy time that go beyond the narrow business considerations that had been the primary focus of the discussion:

Are you going to say that the monied class are the only ones who will have access? . . . Would you then be encouraging, and may we not be seeing . . . a flood of people buying half hours? . . . There is contagion about the use of television, paid television for candidates. They really believe it's magic . . . . Every candidate feels that if he gets on the tube, that equals votes. . . .

He went on to argue for what he characterized as First Amendment rights for the networks on access:

What troubles me is that I have, all my life, believed that the First Amendment really does apply to us as it does to other areas of mass communication. And when you think in First Amendment terms, what you are really saying is that . . . politicians can determine, in this area of the press, access. Whereas if a newspaper of principle . . . decided that they don't want to take a full-page ad to kick off a campaign, because they feel it's too early or because they feel it would distort the process, . . . we would never go to a government agency and then to the courts and say a newspaper can't do it. . . .

Clymer challenged the networks' principled position:

> While I have some sympathy with your feeling that you don't like to be
> regulated by the government, there is a fundamental inconsistency between
> the contention that . . . it was too soon for the campaign to have begun
> from the entertainment side, when very considerable resources had already
> been devoted by the news divisions of all three networks in covering the
> presidential race. They had been chasing around the Florida caucuses.
> They had been doing one thing or another. They had two crews traveling
> with some candidates at some point previous to that message.

Small's response was that the two positions were not inconsistent because they were not taken by the same people; the business side "does not
dictate news decisions either in terms of how we spend our resources or what
we cover."

Robert Zelnick asked R. Brown whether he would apply his principle—
that candidates should be able to buy time whenever and in such time blocks
as they desire—below the presidential level and make it applicable to local
as well as network television. He noted that local television is still relatively
inexpensive in some areas, still a very effective means of communication,
and that there may be dozens of candidates on the ballot. R. Brown responded that "those are interesting concerns," but he declined to comment
on them. Drew asked him whether he would extend the notion of right of
access to political-action committees and, when the question was amended
to include only political-action committees addressing the presidential race,
he said yes. Moderator T. Brown pushed him further, asking him where his
principle came from, what was its "foundation or support?" R. Brown
answered that with respect to the purchase of time on network television by
presidential candidates, the central issue for him was

> who makes those judgments and who the parties are that determine that. I
> guess my response was to being concerned about the networks' making that
> determination based on their perception of how long the campaign season
> ought to be, and how that in fact flies in the face of a candidate's right to get
> his message across at a point in time of strategic importance to him.

R. Brown continued to be pushed. Now Harold Bruno:

> Phil Crane, as a presidential candidate, who happened to announce in the
> summer of 1978, had he the money, should have been able to demand net-
> work time in order to make an announcement in the summer of 1978? . . .

R. Brown answered, "Should he have been able to have been barred by the
networks from doing that? No." Also Lyndon LaRouche and the other
twenty presidential candidates from the other parties, asked Joan Richman?
"Anybody," replied R. Brown.

Segelstein came back in and said,

> I think many of you are kidding yourselves about the audience appetite for this. . . .
>
> Access is very complicated. It is very frustrating to plan your campaign because the mechanics . . . of television are not what they are for the morning show and the evening news. We don't have much live television where you walk into the control room and say to the producer, "Cut the show five minutes short today." . . .
>
> Sure, it's difficult when *we* say when the campaign starts. Somebody has to say when it starts, and I think the first candidate who says it will say it for all, and there will be an immense stampede for air time. . . . The reason we got into it is because other rules and regulations prevent us from saying, "In order to manage this so it best suits the body politic and the larger needs of the public, we won't schedule a program Sunday night at ten or Friday night at eight . . . and we will let that sit there for the politicians to use." . . .

Brown then asked Segelstein what the networks would do with a request from a presidential dark-horse candidate to buy half-hour slots on the network during the ratings period. Segelstein said:

> I think we would have to give serious consideration to the request. I don't know if that particular request is reasonable. We might talk a little, suggest alternatives; . . . candidates are not unreasonable and we are not unreasonable. Some dialogue does take place and time is frequently bought. But I don't know what we would do in May. . . . We are talking about a period in which all the local stations are measured. The networks are measured every day, and they already know how they are doing. But the circulation of the local stations is measured in May, and it could be a serious problem for their sales efforts.

Reasonable Access: Repeal or Interpretation?

Geller argued that despite the Carter/Mondale case, the question of the meaning of the reasonable-access law is not yet settled; or, to be more precise, it could be settled in a new way, to make it more acceptable for all concerned. To lay the groundwork for his proposal, Geller spoke of the reason the law was passed:

> It was enacted because Congress had said that the candidates get the lowest unit rate, and they were afraid then that the broadcasters would beg off affording time. . . . They were protecting themselves, and they said for federal office you have to afford reasonable access or sell reasonable amounts of time. And if you fail to do it, if it is a willful, repeated violation, we will revoke your license. That's all it says. . . .

Geller then argued that the language of the law does not compel the case-by-case approach that the FCC and the networks have favored and that it would be perfectly legal to adopt a longer-range test:

> Look at it overall. If you fail to do it, and it is a willful or repeated violation, then you lose your license at renewal or revocation.

Geller analyzed the disadvantages of the case-by-case handling of requests for time under the reasonable-access law:

> When you go doing it case by case, you get this very deep interference about "is this reasonable?" The candidate always believes he needs it. The network has its views about what the interruption is, what the circumstances are. You are reviewing a judgment here. It's being done by a government agency. It's being done by politically appointed people. Carter/Mondale split four to three, four Democrats and three Republicans. When the case came to the Supreme Court, the Supreme Court said, the reason why you do it on a case-by-case basis is because . . . the networks want that declaratory ruling. Suppose you didn't want it? Suppose the networks came in and said, "We want to be judged overall on whether we have afforded reasonable access?"

Sharp took exception to Geller's proposal, arguing that repeal was a preferable and politically more palatable option:

> We want it repealed because . . . in effect it corrupts the political process rather than helps it.

> Let me give you an example: This [the access requirement] tends to create new access opportunities. For instance, you will recall the candidacy of . . . Ellen McCormack, who had a particular viewpoint on a particular issue. There is no right of access on the basis of that issue. . . . However, by coming in the back door, by declaring candidacy, one-issue candidates can now distort the process by demanding time, on the basis of this statute, to get their views across.

> As for Henry [Geller's] suggestion that we perhaps ought to look at this at renewal time and not look at it on a case-by-case basis, I'm sure that would be acceptable to more broadcasters, probably acceptable to the FCC, but highly unacceptable to the candidates who, having been denied the opportunity to get on the air when they want to get on the air, would say, "Well, I don't care seven years later; I'm getting elected next month."

Geller agreed that the candidates would be unhappy, but

> if that is what the law says, reasonable access, and the legislative history shows it's got to be looked at at renewal, that's it, the candidates are unhappy. You at least have avoided this deep intrusion in journalism and reviewing broadcaster judgment, this First Amendment horror. . . .

> You're not going to get repeal of a statute the politicians like. . . .

Sharp disagreed with Geller's assessment of the likelihood of repeal. He and Small then delved further into the Ellen McCormack case Sharp had raised earlier. Small pointed out that she had qualified for federal funding so that "taxpayers were subsidizing a campaign that was basically her issue, anti-abortion, [with] no serious hope of [her] ever winning a nomination for the presidency. . . ." Sharp added that in addition to taxpayer support for her advertising, the law precludes the networks from censoring or in any way exercising discretion over the content of the ads.

The closing thoughts on reasonable access were offered by Gary Orren. He began by endorsing R. Brown's concern for access for candidates but concluded with support for less regulation:

> The United States is rather unique among industrial democracies in making it difficult for candidates to run for office. We sort of make them jump through hoops. . . .
>
> This is but one of the ways we make it difficult, the question of media access. It is also difficult in the area of campaign finance laws, money. Essentially those laws, at their heart, make it difficult, for many candidates to get involved. . . .
>
> I see this as part of an overall middle class reformer progressive kind of ethos in the United States, which I think is very regrettable. . . .
>
> In this whole area of campaign regulation, I find myself uncharacteristically in agreement with people like Milton Friedman, who would basically just get rid of these regulations and let the political marketplace decide who gets where.

Handling the Presidential Request for Time

George Reedy raised a related issue: How do the networks determine when a president's request for time is political and would trigger obligations under the equal-time law and when it is a presidential report to the people? Leonard tried to respond:

> It's an exceedingly legitimate question, to which there is no firm answer that I've ever been able to figure out.
>
> In the reasonably short time that I've had to wrestle with this, I have been, on at least three or four occasions, greatly troubled by what appeared to be, if one is to take a skeptical or, let's say, perhaps a cynical view of the operation of the White House, that the reason for a particular request for time or a speech is for political purposes, and yet the subject in general is of such importance that it would be arbitrary for a network news executive or a network news division or a network to deny that access.
>
> Furthermore, having granted the request for time, you are then at the mercy of the president as to the use that he puts that time to. A president, of course, very obviously, as you all know, serves two masters, his own

political future—his party, his reelection—and the people in the United States. And sometimes they get mixed up.

I don't know that we always solve it properly. . . . On rare occasions we have denied presidential requests. Presidents put us in the position, more often than not, of making the choice rather than saying, "I command you to give us this time or that time." Sometimes they give us information that makes it possible to make an easy choice, and other times they do not. It is a muddle.

I think, generally, because the three networks operate at that level with goodwill, and probably some common sense—and some fear—the public has not been ill served over the years; and I'm sure the president's purposes have been pretty well served over the years. . . . Everybody does it a little differently. What we have is a policy that says that when the president goes on the air and speaks to a point which is a matter of public controversy, parties—not political parties, but interests—can address themselves to that subject in a reasonably similar time period within a reasonably short space of time . . . and that is our device.

Reedy then raised the issue of a presidential "news conference," which is really just an opportunity for some free and favorable political publicity. Small said that the issue of a response does not arise in the wake of a news conference, however contrived, because

at a news conference, a lot of very able reporters have an opportunity to do follow-ups and catch the president if he has made a statement that is purely propaganda or . . . self-serving.

The Presidential Debates: Who Should Decide?

T. Brown asked Roger Mudd why it was that he, of all the network participants at the conference, appeared to be the only one who seemed to be in favor of retaining the equal-opportunities/equal-time law. His concern, Mudd answered, was for

not the front-runners in the campaign, but the back-runners; and it had been my view that if 315 [Section 315 of the Federal Communications Act, the equal-opportunity law] was eliminated and the networks were then able to dictate the terms of the debates, that those debates would have centered on the two leading candidates, and the back-runners would never have been on the air.

Sharp, who had already indicated his strong support for repeal of Section 315, responded to Mudd:

I share the concern that certain candidates who are not necessarily the first or second candidate in a particular race, however that is measured, might not have their views heard; but I think that there are two points to remember.

One is that if you apply the equal opportunities section to a joint appearance, as you would if the network were the sponsor, not only do you have the first two or the first three or the first four, buy any legally qualified candidates, and those number often in the hundreds.

The second point is this: That is, you are going to have a decision as to who will appear in a joint appearance. I think that what you are going to have to decide is who is going to make the decision. The question is, do you trust a broadcast journalist to make the decision, or do you turn that decision over to another group, or do you have it dictated by government policy? . . .

To put it directly, is the League [of Women Voters] a better person, a better group of people to narrow it to two or three candidates than a network?

Robert MacNeil said there are two questions, the one raised so far is who ought to decide how to limit the number of candidates participating at the debate. But there was a prior issue for him, namely, whether participation should be narrowed at all:

I'm aware of the practical difficulties. I'm just asking, how do you resolve that in terms of the claims of minor parties and less well-known candidates to have access to the principal means of communication?

Leonard commented that, from the network perspective,

the practical answer to the question, if the networks are going to resolve it in the face of a law that says everybody has to be on, is that nobody gets on. So that settles that. So that by default, if you will, and maybe that's the best way to do it, somebody else applies common sense and resolves it in a practical way.

One way or the other, we know . . . that Section 315 is an impractical way to resolve it. So what we're seeking is a practical way to resolve it, . . . to have debates with a reasonable number of candidates. . . .

T. Brown brought the participants back to Mudd's concern that without the equal-opportunities law, non-front runners and third-party candidates may not have access to television.

Bagdikian suggested that the law providing for public financing for presidential candidates has mechanisms for distinguishing between serious, if minor, and nonserious candidates by requiring them to meet some criteria, either through signatures or raising of money, to demonstrate that they have some base of support. He suggested that some similar mechanisms could be developed for distinguishing candidates with respect to eligibility under the equal-time law. Sharp asked whether the standards and determinations about who should qualify for equal time should be made by the government or left to the networks and the broadcast journalists?

Martin Plissner suggested that allowing minor candidates who did not qualify for public financing of their campaigns to participate in debates would hardly make up for the disadvantage they suffered by the lack of funding. Edwin Diamond proposed that once candidates had crossed some eligibility threshold, broadcast journalists could hold a debate among the front runners and one among the back runners. Bruno wondered whether anyone would watch a debate among the also-rans. And Stuart Loory asked if such a system were adopted, whether a back runner could ever become a front runner.

Geller sided with those who wanted to see the government out of the business of regulating appearances by presidential candidates:

> I would trust the judgment of the broadcaster to begin with. You can get reports on how it works out. If there are abuses, you can take action. But the government shouldn't intervene until they see the abuses.

> There have been proposals, if you want mechanistic ones, . . . to use a percentage, a very low percentage that brings everybody who is significant within equal time. You can use a figure of two percent generated by the party in the previous election and one percent on petitions.

> But what I am saying is that whatever the percentage is, it would be one chosen to include anybody significant, but to get out the vegetarians and the others who have no real significance in the process. . . .

> It worked out very well in 1960. It has worked out other times very well. I would ask for reports from the FCC and others; and then if it continued to work out well, I would leave it alone and simply repeal it for president and vice president.

> It is a different issue . . . when you get to local races.

Clymer wondered why the networks wanted this responsibility:

> I can understand very much why you don't want the government telling you you may not sponsor debates and decide who is in them, . . . why you must be uninvolved with the League of Women Voters. . . .

> Why do you want to be involved? Why do you not want to cover other people's news events? Why do you want the responsibility for saying this guy is serious and this guy isn't? Isn't the journalist's job not to make news but to cover it?

Wald said that Clymer's newspaper, the *New York Times*, tried to arrange debates in the 1980 presidential election. Clymer said that is was discussed at the *Times*, and Leonard and Bruno added that the *Des Moines Register* had staged a debate in Iowa and a paper in New Hampshire had done the same thing there. Clymer responded by saying that he still did not think it was the right thing to do and reiterated his question, why not stick to covering news "that is out there" rather than creating it? Brokaw said they wanted to do both. Bruno said that the issue was journalistic discretion and that they just wanted to be free to exercise "the same editorial judgments that any other journalists exercise."

Mudd added what appeared to be a note of basic realism to the discussion:

> I think one possible answer to your question . . . is that a debate, for instance, between the two leading candidates, the ones that we all know and most of us follow, is a much more interesting broadcast than to have it cluttered up with five or six or seven other minor candidates. It is less exciting, probably, and I think it is easier for the networks to deal with technically and from a program standpoint, with just the two big guns.

Clymer pointed out that the debate-coverage problem was one reason for repealing Section 315 for the presidential and vice-presidential campaigns, but he did not respond to the issue of why the networks wanted to get in the business of sponsoring debates.

Geller pointed out that the equal-opportunity law also prevents local broadcasters from staging local debates:

> The FCC has reported, and I think correctly, that this may be inhibiting full coverage of the campaign by restricting the broadcaster from making his contribution. . . . You are undermining having a fully informed electorate.

> It is a phony restriction. It is still a bona fide news event, whether it is . . . put on by the *New York Times* or CBS and NBC and ABC.

T. Brown turned to Dot Ridings who earlier had indicated being in favor of retaining the equal-time law. She said that the League of Women Voters has had more experience running debates at the state and local, rather than the national, levels and that they have found

> great relief and gratitude that the local affiliates do . . . turn it over to somebody else to organize, structure and present as an event which they then come to cover as news. . . .

> I'm uncomfortable . . . with either real or perceived judgments being placed by news organizations on the inclusion of those kinds of candidates, . . . What really elevates a non-major party contender for any office, what gives that person the right to become a major contender, and who makes those kinds of decisions. . . .

Warren Mitofsky pressed her on the adequacy of the league's decisions on including independent candidate John Anderson in the 1980 debates. She answered that no one at the league was "totally comfortable" with it and characterized their standard as "the best" of a collection of "imperfect solutions." Professor Neustadt asked her why she would not prefer a news organization, which has "a great deal of experience in these sorts of judgments," to the league? She argued that the league has been in the debate-sponsoring business longer than television, although she acknowledged that the issues were troubling ones. Segelstein wondered whether it would not be better to have three organizations making those decisions, on the theory that they might very likely make different ones and "the problems might be offset from one organization to the other."

T. Brown asked Congressman Obey whether he would prefer the networks to the league as debate organizers. He replied that

> while I am not at all fond of the format . . . that the league adopted on presidential races, and I think a lot of times the league gets in the way of really having true confrontations between the candidates (or are used in order to avoid true confrontations between the candidates), I still in the last analysis am somewhat more comfortable with the unbiased credentials of the league than I am a number of local broadcasters.

Congressman Obey did indicate that he would be "less concerned" if Section 315 were repealed only for presidential candidates rather than for all candidates.

Small returned to the network perspective:

> It isn't that we don't love the League of Women Voters, and it isn't that we would not carry a debate that they sponsored. In the final analysis, as we saw by the experience of 1980, it is the candidates who decide which forum they will go with . . . if the candidates chose only to go to a debate . . . sponsored by the Boy Scouts of America, we would cover it. What we object to is . . . excluding networks from becoming sponsors.

Small criticized the ruling by the FCC (the so-called Aspen decision) that defined debates by sponsors such as the League cf Women Voters as "bona fide news events" and therefore excluded them from the equal-time obligations imposed by Section 315. In that decision, the FCC also ruled that a broadcaster-sponsored debate would not be so defined. The theory behind the FCC decision was that it is not a news event if the medium covering it also staged it. Small pointed out that in the first presidential debate of 1980, in Philadelphia, the debate stopped as soon as there were broadcast audio problems. "If it was a bona fide debate," he asked, "why the hell didn't they just continue debating?" And if the test of bona fideness is nonstaging, Small continued, then it follows that interviews conducted by the networks with leading political figures should not be bona fide news events either. In response to the Philadelphia story, Ridings pointed out that the sound system in the auditorium was tied into the broadcast sound system; thus when the audio went out on the airwaves, it went out in the auditorium too, and that accounted, at least in part, for why the debate stopped. Small rebutted by recounting his own experience at that debate when he said that he could hear the moderator very well from his seat far away from the stage while the broadcast audio was still off.

Ridings returned to Small's earlier charge that the candidates really dictated the conditions of the debates, particularly the question of the

Photo by Martha Stewart

Left to right: Congressman David Obey, D-Wisconsin (back to camera); Richard B. Wirthlin, President, Decision/Making/Information; Judy Woodruff, White House Correspondent, NBC News; John Deardourff, Chairman of the Board, Bailey, Deardourff and Associates; and Gary Orren, Associate Professor of Public Policy, John F. Kennedy School of Government.

inclusion of Anderson. Ridings said that the Anderson question had been assessed on a week-by-week basis and that at the beginning of the week of the final negotiations for the debate, he no longer met the criteria for inclusion. She agreed with Bruno's suggestion that Reagan may have come to debate terms that week because Anderson was out and he then wanted a one-on-one confrontation with Carter, but she reiterated her point that the decision to exclude Anderson was based on standards that had been in place and in use for several months.

Drew then focused the discussion on the issue that had been underlying the last exchange between Small and Ridings:

> A real question in the whole area of debates is not whether television organizations manage it or the league manages it, but to what degree the candidates themselves are succeeding in managing it and manipulating it. . . .

> Was it healthy to have only one debate in 1980, as close as possible to the election as one camp could get, therefore allowing for as little time for analysis as possible. . . ?

She wondered whether the networks would allow the candidates' camps to approve the panelists? Bruce Morton argued that the candidates are always going to push for conditions that they perceive to be in their best interests, no matter who is running the debate. Drew countered that it would be possible to "build in a kind of pressure and expectation that 'if you want your debates, fellows, here are the rules.' " Bruno agreed with Drew:

> The candidates have really distorted the debates in many ways. At one point, many of us were asked for opinions on how the debates should be staged, and I think everybody agreed that the ideal thing would be to have the candidates face each other with only a moderator, not to have this panel of news people, which really in effect turns it into a glorified press conference.

> Every single time, my understanding is, it has been the candidates who refused to do it that way, to have a real debate, and insisted on having us there as panelists as sort of a security blanket for them.

Morton also favored having no panel of journalists.

Reedy and Obey reiterated their concern that while they had few objections to repealing Section 315 for presidential candidates, they were very concerned about the idea of repeal across the board. Reedy argued that in small markets, it was likely that there are "station owners and also news editors who are probably rather deeply plunged into the process of local politics." Congressman Obey added that once there was a partial repeal, local broadcasters would be sure to push for the next step and, "it is damn hard, if that is the only major media outlet in town, to stand up to those people." Sharp responded to those concerns:

I have two answers. . . .

The first answer is the easy one, and that is I really don't expect to see that much abuse. . . .

Second, . . . I think the important thing is that, with respect to the First Amendment, it is a fundamental freedom, it is essential to the workings of a democratic society, and that to the extent there might be some abuse, you have to take the risk of abuse to reach for that higher value. You have to assume that risk. You have to be willing to take that chance. That's what democracy is all about.

"What about the First Amendment right of the candidates to be heard," Congressman Obey asked, "or are they just supposed to speak down into black holes?"
Sharp answered that

when the first Congress met and enacted the first ten amendments, the nature of that act was to prevent the government from preventing speech, and to prevent government from interfering with the right of the press, not to create rights for people to hear.

Now, you may argue that it is somewhat empty if you can't hear it, but that was not the intent of the framers. . . .

Bagdikian suggested that "in practical terms," Sharp was underestimating

the number of communities, including a number of House districts, in which there is a dominant paper, and the percentage of those which have refused ads on a partisan basis, political ads, and who also own the leading radio or television outlet in the community, and have similarly treated opposing candidates unfairly. I don't think it is a random occurence; I think it is a significant one.

Tom Brokaw disagreed:

How many of those stations exist around the country? How many of those situations exist in communities around the country . . . where candidates are locked out of the process in a growing communication marketplace that we now have, where they have access to not just television, but to cable, to radio, to any number of things? . . .

The fact is that in most communities that I experience as I travel around the country, large and small, there is a terrific competitive nature now to get people on the air, not to hold them off the air. . . .

If you have real statistical data that show that twenty-eight percent of the stations in the country controlled by newspapers deny access, then I think your argument has real merit, . . . but if you are making your conclusions based on the same intuitive thinking that Mr. Sharp is, I just don't think it holds water. . . .

Bagdikian answered Brokaw by saying that he "didn't have any data" but that he thought Brokaw was overestimating the efficiency of reaching the community with alternative sources:

> It is true, in five, ten, fifteen years, there may be a very large number of alternative ways. It is not true today, and candidates who have a choice between having a big ad in a newspaper, getting access to the first, second or third radio or TV station, have no question that it is much more effective to do that than to buy time on a cable or on a number of cable outlets.

Brokaw responded by arguing that there were "very few communities in this country, or none that I know of . . . where they would lock out a candidate in a community of any size at all." In addition, he said that there are very few communities where one outlet "owns the marketplace."

What would Brokaw think if it were a problem, asked T. Brown?

Brokaw urged suspending Section 315 for presidential campaigns, "see how it works and go from there and work it down." Brokaw said that he had

> faith in the communications marketplace that is now evolving in this country. . . . If you go around the country now and go to these communities, you will find that you can have access to a number of outlets that have almost equal weight.

Geller suggested that there were practical political obstacles to outright repeal of Section 315 that argued strongly for an "evolutionary" approach, that is, beginning the repeal process with only presidential campaigns at first. He urged that equal time should be retained for a while with respect to paid time for all other elections. Then he recommended an experiment with free time for nonpresidential elections: Why not suspend 315 and use the fairness doctrine as a back-up? The fairness doctrine requires fair, not strictly equal, treatment of issues in a broadcaster's overall programming. Geller was suggesting that

> if a broadcaster acts in a way that truly is distorting the process by favoring one candidate by taking actions that show a flagrant pattern,

then the FCC could proceed against that station under the fairness doctrine.

Afterword

The session on regulatory issues generated the sharpest differences between the networks and the politicians of the entire conference. After all, the laws were enacted by politicians, and they serve their interests; the broadcasters would prefer, for both journalistic and business reasons, to be left alone.

On reasonable access, most of the discussion centered on the implications of the Supreme Court decision in the Carter/Mondale case, holding that there was a right under the law to buy a half-hour of prime time to announce a campaign for the presidency in December preceding the election year. The networks said that such a policy was unfair from a business point of view, was a journalistic intrusion that would not be acceptable on the print side from a First Amendment point of view, and did not take into account that there were other ways for the candidates to get their messages across. The networks warned that early-time buys that disrupted the regular entertainment schedule would be unpopular and would backfire on the candidates. For their parts, the politicians argued that at the heart of the democratic-election process is the importance of the candidate's being able to communicate with the voters. That interest simply could not be served if the networks could refuse to sell time because they were free to make the judgment, in effect overruling the candidate, that on the business side of the network at least, the campaign had not yet begun.

Some of those not directly involved worried about the financial implications of Carter/Mondale: Would the wealthy and well-financed have an undue advantage if the television-advertising campaign could start earlier and earlier and with larger blocks of time? And some of the network people wondered whether the next election would see an increasing number of one-issue, nonparty presidential candidates using reasonable access to gain visibility for their views more than for themselves as serious candidates.

As a middle ground, Geller suggested that the law could be reinterpreted, without congressional sanction, to require FCC evaluation of a licensee's performance only at renewal time rather than on a case-by-case basis. However, the politicians would not be happy with such a situation since their interest would be in the current election, not in a licensee's overall performance.

On equal opportunity, the dialogue centered on the question of debates; again the core question seemed to be whether the networks, the politicians, the government, or a "disinterested" party such as the League of Women Voters should call the shots. Most of the broadcasters favored outright repeal, although Mudd expressed concern for the impact of repeal on non-front runners and minor-party candidates. The only other argument against repeal seemed to be the notion that journalists should be reporting, not staging, news events, but several participants pointed out that, right or wrong, newspapers have been sponsoring debates for years. Once again, a middle ground emerged: There was broad consensus, somewhat reluctant from some quarters, that it was in everyone's interest and in the public interest to suspend the law for the presidential and vice-presidential candidates. There was some hope expressed that this partial suspension would generate more debates and considerable pressure on the candidates to participate and that it would reduce the degree to which the candidates could dictate the formats. More debates with different sponsorships might result in different formats, and that was seen to be a healthy consequence both because it would test out alternatives and would cancel out an advantage one candidate might have in a particular system. There was lots of speculation and little agreement on what might happen at the local level if equal opportunity were simply repealed, but there was enough uncertainty and concern that only the hardiest deregulators were willing to push that position.

This session was different from the rest. The entire landscape was not covered, but the issues were discussed in considerable depth. The differences among the participants were great, the lines were sharply drawn, and the participants were able to argue from hard-nosed practical realities as well as broader perspectives. For each of the two central questions on the floor, middle positions were developed. Geller's proposal to reinterpret reasonable access has now been reflected in a petition filed with the FCC. And perhaps the broad support or partial suspension of equal opportunity will contribute to congressional attention and even perhaps White House support early enough in the political season to ensure a richer debate experience for the candidates and for the people in coming elections.

7

Wrap-up and Reflections

The final session of the conference was held after lunch on Sunday. It was designed to provide the opportunity to listen to Massachusetts Institute of Technology political scientist Ithiel deSola Pool, who had been asked to observe the entire proceedings and share his thoughts on what he had heard; to enable those who had not spoken much during the weekend to share their views; to give some of the more active participants a chance to reflect on what had taken place; and to raise issues that had not been covered earlier.

The comments were varied and random. Some addressed the larger structural issues of the television industry and of the relationship of the networks to the presidential campaigns. Others focused on more specific topics.

The speeches, edited from the transcript of the conference, have been reproduced here in the order in which they were delivered at this final session. Both because of what the speakers say and because of who the speakers are, the following comments constitute an important part of the conference and of this book, and they provide a very fitting and appropriate final chapter.

Ithiel deSola Pool

The goal of the meeting was not to adopt codes or resolutions or reach conclusions. But out of this kind of frank interchange, conducted with civility, comes an internalization of awareness of various problems and of their social consequences; out of that grows better professional practice. This meeting has been of that character. It has produced interaction with tolerance that is hard to achieve, but is an effective condition for the functioning of a democratic decision process.

No sort of consensus has emerged. At any kind of convention or meeting, the most important things are what happens in the corridors. So I conducted a kind of corridor poll. I went to a representative sample of the people present and asked them a question: "We have talked about a lot of things, but what one problem most bothers you about the way things are now, what is there that something ought to be done about whether it is done by government, by the media themselves, or whomever it may be?" I got a variety of replies.

What was most interesting was the total absence of any convergence. One person told me, "Nothing"; he said he is satisfied with the present situation. A second person said no one big thing, maybe twenty or thirty little things, but nothing that he could single out as particularly important.

Another person mentioned the exit polls and their effects in California. Another person talked about gavel-to-gavel coverage. Another person said it was what's going to happen when Anderson shows up with $6 million in 1984. Another person mentioned Section 315, which did receive a lot of discussion on the floor.

Another person mentioned the need for going to one hour of news as the most important single thing they would like to see discussed. One person mentioned the question of how the media can themselves take on the responsibility of bringing issues into analysis, even if the candidates don't do it.

It is the last of these that comes closest to what concerned me most, namely, the intense focus in our whole discussion on campaign strategy. I fear I will be misunderstood if I make some remarks here, as I will, deploring the focus on the horse race rather than on issues. It may be read as an attack upon what the networks are doing; and an attack upon TV. That is not what I am trying to say.

It is a condition that I deplore, but, as Robert MacNeil said, it is inevitable. It is the product of the short time available for the treatment of the material, and that short time does not lend itself to a systematic analysis of issues.

It is a product of the politicians' running the campaigns. In most cases, they do not want real issues brought to a head. The issues that they would like to talk about are essentially motherhood issues, which are chosen for a strategic emphasis, but they don't want to answer what others might consider to be the hard questions.

It is a product also of what the audience is interested in. So it is a product of many things. What I am not saying is that there is something wrong with the decisions being made by the media to focus on the horse race; rather, what I want to bring out is something about the structure of the way we all think about these problems.

A conference on television and elections could have been organized with an agenda that asked such questions as, how can a television system be designed and structured so as to best raise the information level of the public? How can a television system be organized so as to clarify questions about public policy? What kind of television would change the motivation structure of candidates and lead them to see an advantage for themselves in talking more about issues and more seriously?

Or one could even ask, what kind of television system would lead to a re-creation and rebuilding of the old type of political parties which involved the public in the political process in a way that nothing now does?

Such normative questions could have been the agenda of a meeting that was called "Television and Elections." But instead, what did we actually do?

According to the way in which this meeting was conceptualized, we started out by going through a hypothetical strategic planning exercise. We took the existing structure as given; we took the system as given, and simply said—as our master of ceremonies turned to one person and then to another—If you were up in the cabin on the mountain, what would you do? How would you use television? What would be your next step?

So the politicians were asked what they wanted television to do as a strategic matter. We were repeatedly asked how we might go about getting the particular kind of television coverage that one wanted.

Even in our own academic thinking about the problem, we defined the problem as essentially a horse race problem, we defined the problem as a strategic problem, and it shouldn't surprise us at all that other people think the same way.

That sheds some light on fundamental reasons why we get Professor Robinson's three-to-one and four-to-one ratios. It is so much a part of our culture that we take the system for granted and look at it as a game. The word *game* has been applied to politics for many years. There is an old book by Frank Kent, *The Great Game of Politics*. We look at politics as a game, even in our intellectual analysis; we ask the questions in this strategic way.

Perhaps, at some future meetings or in research studies by the organization that is developing here, at the Institute of Politics, there will be attempts made to ask some of the larger structural kinds of questions that I have pointed to—to ask questions such as what kind of television system would provide a focus on the big picture and help citizens to understand better the nature of the political process.

Walter Lippmann wrote a classic, *Public Opinion*, which was a book about the media of his day; namely, the newspapers. His central question was not just what newspapers do right and wrong, although he talked about that a lot, but what is necessary for there to be an intelligent public opinion in a democratic society. He concluded that the newspapers can't do that job by themselves. In his words, they shed a beam of light on the problem, a narrow beam. They do not look at it broadly and with depth.

I'm not sure that he had all the right answers. Essentially what he was arguing for was establishing think tanks, getting political scientists to look at problems, as well as newspapers. While I'm not sure what is the right answer, at least he was asking the right question. That is the question that I don't think we reached in this meeting. Because he asked the right question and discussed it intelligently, his book is a classic.

What I have been talking about so far is what we have not discussed at this meeting. I do not intend to try to summarize all the wise things that have been said. I am talking around them. There were other things that we did not discuss at this meeting that I might just note briefly.

For example, except for an opening set of remarks by Anthony Oettinger on the first evening of the meeting, there was very little attention to technological changes. That may be quite appropriate if our focus is on 1984 because the election of 1984 is not going to be that drastically different from the election of 1980; the media system is going to be very much as it was.

The possibility that campaigns will be putting out material that is not broadcast over the air, but over cable, was never mentioned at all, as far as I could see. I don't think there will be an enormous amount of that in 1984, but by 1988 it will probably be a significant thing.

One thing that finally came up in this morning's discussion that I would like to emphasize further, was the fact that the new technologies are undermining many of the assumptions that justified regulation in the past.

Mr. Wald said that regulation is based upon a view of the technology that is becoming outmoded. And he gave us a hypothetical story, somewhat fanciful of course, of the *Wall Street Journal's* losing a court case because it transmits its text by satellite to the distributed print plants. But it is true that broadcasting is no longer a very special case separate and apart from the print media, which needs to have a special regime of its own because of scarcity of spectrum.

The First Amendment implications of current broadcast regulations are not just what 315 does. The First Amendment issues are diffusing as the technology of electronic transmission is itself also diffusing in ways that interconnect the problems of the print media and the broadcasting media. Which pattern will we choose—the pattern that came from the tradition of print, or the pattern that came from the tradition of early broadcasting, conditioned by the notion of spectrum shortage, a notion that of course is becoming more and more obsolete?

So much for things that we didn't discuss or, in the last case, that just began to surface. I'd like to take the last few moments by noting some of the points that were made that were to me highlights of the session.

I was particularly impressed by the extraordinary first afternoon session, when Floyd Abrams was acting as the cross-examiner and asked our media participants to say what bothered them. He brought out a whole series of problems that were on the minds of people present. In fact, the TV people said everything that is cited by critics from the outside, but did it with much more expertise, much more balance, and much more insight into the nature of the problems than the outside critic is likely to bring to bear.

William Leonard traced the origins of some of these dilemmas to the history of print, the history of radio, and to the structure of competition in the industry. Robert MacNeil noted the inferiority feelings that he said broadcast journalists sometimes have in regard to their print colleagues, the feeling that newspaper reporters have an opportunity to dig more, and the psychological consequences that he saw of this difference in their roles.

Elizabeth Drew noted the negative tone that she said robs the political process of a sense of majesty, and the tendency to run down whoever gets into the limelight. This was affirmed in discussion by various people from the TV industry itself. Roger Mudd referred to the desire of TV reporters not to be seen by their colleagues as being taken in.

Robert MacNeil expressed the feeling that the political process was cheapened by the briefness of the commercial message. Not everyone agreed, of course, but no one really offered any very strong reasons for not liking the idea of allowing the five-minute piece. The half-hour piece also got a good deal of discussion. But I couldn't find any clear-cut arguments presented against the five-minute political statement.

Now, I'm not saying that these self-critical remarks are the whole truth, certainly not, nor necessarily that everybody agrees with them entirely. Many important points were made about the process by which TV news reporting has been improving, and the ways in which it has improved the political process.

I single out the self-critical remarks because it is indeed unusual and a testimony to the environment of candor and trust that evolved in this meeting that people were ready and willing to bare the things that were on their minds, stating their concerns so openly. Clearly, many of these concerns have some basis. Clearly, much that was said in self-criticism is right, and in the answers, likewise.

Lewis Wolfson

The one thing that I missed here, was a follow-up to what Liz Drew said about how the media set the tone for the voters, and therefore set, in effect, the attitude of the voter. Do we think enough about that? Do we set up a system of covering campaigns—and here we're talking about television— without having a vehicle for really assessing on a regular basis how campaigns are going to be covered in the future and correcting the mistakes that have been made in the past?

I would have liked to have heard what the system is at the networks in particular for reassessing this. I know it is a cliché; I know that journalists are tired of being studied and raked over. We say, "See the mistakes you made in 1976," and they say, "Yes, we're not going to make them in 1980." Maybe they don't make the same mistakes in 1980, but they make other mistakes. Is there enough consideration at the networks of how to correct those mistakes and develop a system for reassessing?

Adam Clymer

I have a few thoughts jotted down, and I guess part of the interest for me, in this whole process, has been looking at the television people.

I look at you in two ways, and they conflict. On the one hand, you are colleagues and friends, in many cases, and on the other hand, you are players, and one doesn't want to get too close to players in covering politics. I guess you are more like colleagues. I mean, one hears the same alternation of doubts, some that seem well founded and some that don't, and some smugness that would make Jimmy Carter seem humble, just the way one does in any newspaper office that I ever worked in; we heard all of that in the course of this session.

Obviously, to a degree we are all players, if we write for a newspaper that anyone reads or appear on television or radio stations with anything but the most trivial audiences. And some things that we do in the newspaper business or in the television business, in the most obvious pursuit of reporting, inevitably will have an effect, short or long, on the campaign.

Far more often in listening to these discussions, I have heard people talking about how they do business, what they think they do well, what they think they might do better, and that sounds like colleagues. When you want to be free of the FCC's restrictions that say you may not stage a debate, then you are sounding like colleagues.

But when you say you want to go ahead and stage the debate and set the rules, then I am concerned that it is not quite how I would want it done, if I were in charge of something. But you have a perfect right to make that decision, and the government shouldn't tell you you can't. I caution, though, that I think this is one of the areas where you may invite being players, without thinking about it as much as you can.

I'm really not qualified to comment on the quality of the reporting that people do. I've been around it, and I know that it is shorter than most stories I write, but I know that it is hard work to do it well. Shorter is by no means easier. I worked for three months at the *New York Daily News*, which is an adventure, and trying to convey sixty percent of what you could convey in a thousand words in two hundred words is a good test. That's the kind of test that most of the good television and radio correspondents are meeting in a slightly different form every day. So I admire that.

There is one thing that I think you do as players that does concern me about the system, and that is when you get involved right at the point of voting.

When CBS tells people who has won in the Maine caucuses when a third of them haven't been conducted, there is a consequence; there is a risk that you affect what happens in the last third of the voting. When you broadcast not that so and so has won the election before the polls close, but when you broadcast at five or six or seven o'clock in the afternoon, before the polls have closed in a lot of the country, there is a substantial risk.

No, it hasn't been proved, but there is a substantial risk that you discourage people in the West, and because Democrats vote later, more likely Democrats, from bothering to vote. Now, there is no way that anyone could argue that this would affect the presidential outcome, but there is a reasonably good suspicion, unproven by any data, that it affects the outcome of state and local elections. And I think those are important.

I'm not arguing that you must not do any of these things, but I am arguing that I don't think that you think hard enough about the consequences of some of the things that you do. I think sessions like this are useful, and I hope that you all think about some of these impacts, particularly when you become players, a little bit more than I think you do.

David Webster

What I was fascinated by is the difference, rightly or wrongly, in the way in which in different countries we have addressed essentially the same problems, or very similar problems, even accepting enormous structural differences both in the political and the broadcasting systems.

Here, unmediated access by candidates to time in broadcasting is a purchased commodity, which is typical of the system anyhow, which is essentially a commercial enterprise. But to many Europeans, particularly the British, the idea of purchasing time as a form of political advertising would be anathema. In fact, it is not only anathema, it is illegal. So we don't have that problem.

Also, you were much more hesitant about the idea of ganging up to deal with the problem. You have these curious antitrust laws, and it somehow inhibits you from actually getting together and saying, "There is a problem; let's sort it out." You are like wrestlers, and you're wrestling in the mud, and everybody is trying to gain advantage; but there are no rules to the wrestling match, and nobody is even quite sure what the extent of the arena is.

William Leonard

(Leonard began by asking Pool to state "the fundamental unasked question of the conference." Pool responded by saying that "what we did not get to was the question of what kind of a television structure would produce a more informed electorate and a more intelligent discussion of public issues. . . . That question simply was put aside." "Well," Leonard commented, "that gives us a very good excuse for the next conference.")

I would like to address myself to the question about getting together. Networks are tempted to get together, I suspect, and the one time that we did get together was at a time when the process of collecting the so-called raw vote—this goes back to 1964—had gotten to the point where the three networks had 75,000 precinct reporters, on a particular night in June, in the State of California, attempting to discover whether Goldwater had beaten Rockefeller or vice versa.

As a result of that, and when each wire service had eleven reporters trying to find out the same thing, there developed something called the News Election Service.

It took a very grudging, a very grudging letter from the Justice Department to allow the two wire services and the three networks to supply, on election night, such a service, and only on the condition that we then go ahead, independently, and produce estimates in advance of that, or estimate independently, which we have done. We now have another whole set of estimates, and some people have suggested that they provide more confusion than enlightenment; and upon those estimates, we now have exit polling, a third level.

As one of the early developers of all of this very expensive process (the total cost of which is something in the order of $5 million a network on each election night), I must say that the sum total of information is simply to inform the public five or six hours earlier than they would know anyway.

If I had it all to do over again, I'm not sure that that is the right emphasis for our effort. That amount of money is very large, and my thought would be that somehow we should devise some more sensible, more understandable, less expensive, and more common sense way to develop, even if we had to do it noncompetitively, the results of election night. Because I'm not sure that the enormous effort and ingenuity and talent that is applied to it—I sound like a reformed drunk here, and I guess I am—is worth the candle.

I think we could well apply that kind of money, that kind of effort, to an improvement to our coverage of the campaign, obviously of our coverage of the issues, and of our coverage, certainly, of the primaries.

I also believe that history, time, and pride in exercising our ability as reporters resulted, many years ago, in the enormous coverage that we give the conventions. The convention as a political instrumentality has changed over the years. We have not caught up with that change.

We have covered the change, which is basically that the primaries have become the first through twelfth ballot or fifteenth ballot, but we still continue to make an effort at the conventions that I do not believe is warranted, and I don't think that the public, which kind of turns its back on it, feels it is warranted either. I'm not sure that even serious political observers feel that it is warranted.

Again, I would hope that over the years, assuming that the conventions continue to be what they are now, a kind of a blessing on what has happened during the primaries, that we would take that enormous amount of money at the network level, $10 million a network, something like that, and apply it in some other and more fruitful fashion.

I hope that my successors and others will examine these two areas, in the hope that we can in totality do a better job in the future.

On the whole, though, I must say that I think I'm exceedingly proud, exceedingly proud, not only of CBS's efforts over the years, but of all the efforts of the other two networks. If there was ever an area in journalism that we have taken seriously for thirty years, if there was ever an effort in which our management has met its responsibilities, it is in the area of meeting, to the best of our abilities, and they have been considerable abilities, our responsibilities in the area of political coverage.

We have done our darndest, without hope of much return and sometimes in the face of great criticism, to apply the very best effort, the very best people, the very largest amounts of money, year after year after year. And in total, I think the record of the three news divisions and the networks in this arena is perhaps the very proudest record that we have to display.

Robert MacNeil

I know I probably irritate my colleagues on the commercial networks by being the kind of chronic kvetch; and sitting where I do in a kind of ivory tower in public television, it is safe for me to do that. But I think that Professor Pool has a point in saying that we continue to take all the system for granted.

I was impressed by the way the veil of complacency was drawn aside a little bit by my commercial network colleagues, and I don't mean personal complacency, because I don't think that any one of them I know suffers from that. But there is a kind of institutional complacency and arrogance which has gone with the enormous power and position that you have all had over the years, which may now begin to be eroded a little bit as your sort of hegemony, as the Chinese say, is perhaps going to change.

It was very refreshing to hear that, but I think from both that and the people we might call the manipulators, there was an element of disingenuousness, because the manipulators got away I think with outrageous oversimplifications of their roles. They were pretending that access was very difficult and they were reduced to these tiny messages, implying strongly that the content of those messages was nothing by truth and beauty and enlightenment.

They are called manipulators rightly, because they are trying to package and create impressions about candidates based on imagery and all the techniques that have become so sophisticated.

I think, if I may say with respect about my network colleagues, they were being a little bit disingenuous themselves, by implying that the brevity of time given to individual stories in newscasts was somehow immutable and a law handed down with the creation of television, as though General Sarnoff, wherever he is, had handed some tablets down on which it is said that stories can only be certain lengths. That is all arbitrary.

They can change, as NBC demonstrated when they introduced Segment Three some years ago and decided to devote three or five minutes to an individual story. It can all be changed, as the networks demonstrate every night on the nightly news when there is a really big story running; with various aspects of that story they sometimes consume a third or two-thirds of their entire newscast. It is all arbitrary, and it can be changed.

I think it is because, in the anxiety to keep the maximum audience attendant and keep the eyeballs glued, an awful lot of the production effort goes into retaining the interest or the attention of the uninterested; if some more concern were paid to informing or making comprehensible issues, I think there might be an improvement.

I agree with Bill Leonard that the system is a system that already serves the viewer, by and large, very well in terms of informing him of the democracy. It is just that existing at the margin of it as I do, I think it could be moderately better.

I just think that in the new competition that started in 1980 and is going to exist among the three networks and become, I suppose, even more aggressive, some part might be used to look for new ways to do things, whether it is simply longer segments or whether there are actually new program forms that could be created and devoted exclusively to the coverage of politics.

I think the system is terrifically impressive the way it is, and I just hunger to see things somewhat improved on the edges, and I don't think all the forms have yet been discovered. If I can be sightly immodest about it, I think that the form we have created on public television is a small demonstration of alternative forms which can be used in this wonderful medium to help inform people.

George Reedy

I wanted to start out with something of a cautionary note that goes back to many, many years studying semantics. That is, all through this conference, I have heard a few words used that everyone thinks they understand, that I rather suspect are not being defined precisely and are being defined differently in different minds. And the one word that I think is being abused the most is the word *issue*. There is an assumption here that we all mean the same thing when we say that the networks are not informing the people of the issues. I rather think they are informing the people of the issues in which they are interested.

It seems to me that the American electorate, in comparison with other countries that I have been in, and in comparison to other places where I have seen elections, is really rather well informed.

There is another point here. I am not so certain that I want to hear our political leaders going through a lot of lengthy analyses of what they are going to do. Let's be a little bit realistic. Number one, these men don't know what they are going to do after they get elected. For the love of God, we do not give them the authority to do anything.

What we give a president of the United States is the right to negotiate with the Congress, to negotiate with the courts, to negotiate with the state governments, to negotiate with all of the peer groups in our society as to how the country is going to be run.

Most of you must be familiar with what happened to Franklin Delano Roosevelt when he made his speech in Pittsburgh announcing that he was going to cut the budget by twenty-five percent—this was in 1932—and a few months later, the Republicans started calling attention to this particular promise. He called in Judge Sam Rosenman and said, "Sam, how can I explain this?" Rosenman came back the next day and said, "Mr. President, the only way you can explain that speech is to deny you ever made it."

In the first place, these men do not know what they are going to do; that's number one. Number two is I do not believe that the political campaign is any place for a deep discussion of issues. I think we do get a deep discussion of issues in the American system. I think we get it after the election. I think we get it when the issues become real, when they are presented to Congress where they can be analyzed the way issues should be analyzed.

You know, one of the things that you learn if you work in a senatorial office, which I did for quite some time, is that the most fallacious myth is that there are two sides to every issue. There are not. There are 2,200 sides to every issue, and the kind of simplistic speech which is absolutely essential in a campaign is not devoted, in my judgment, to anything, any analysis of issues that is deeper than slogans.

What are the American people interested in in a campaign? You know, I believe the American people are somewhat more sophisticated about our system than we give them credit for. I think there is a tendency to underrate their intelligence simply because they do not use the same language that those of us use who are professionals in the English language. I think that they understand that there are certain overriding issues which do come through, and that also what is really important is the character and the philosophy of the people that are running. I suspect that they make rather good choices.

You know, it is fashionable to cite some of the clunks that we have had for president, and we have had some duds; there is no question about that. But have you ever looked at the people they defeated?

What I have heard here, as when I heard Roger Mudd the other day, are statements that sounded precisely like the things that my father and the newspaper men around him were saying in the 1920s about their profession. It sounds precisely like the things that I said when I was a very young reporter, exercising a lot of shoe leather around the United States Senate.

I suspect that this is the kind of thing that is going on at all times, and I think it is very healthy, because I think this kind of thing will impel people to do better. But that is a different thing than leaping to the conclusion that reporters are not doing the job of covering issues.

I believe they are covering the issues. I think they are covering the only issues that people are interested in; and I think that what you will do, if you ever do get politicians into the kind of issue analysis we are talking about, is just lead to a lot of disappointing promises.

I do not think the American system is set up that way. This is not a parliamentary system where you can rely upon a political party with a set of promises to at least make an effort to carry them out once it gets into power. We do not live under that system, and I think we have to take our system for what it is.

My closing remarks are this: It seems to me that there is a process of social evolution. You know, Darwinism has repercussions in the political field just as well as it does in the biological field. And one of the things that has happened to our political system and to our method of reporting is that what we have has resulted from certain evolutionary processes. It continues, it gets a little bit better all the time, I think. It can still get better.

I think we can do the same sort of mental process with this question of covering the issues. They are never going to be covered satisfactorily enough. How satisfactory is satisfactory? How far can a dog run into the woods?

Stuart Loory

First of all, I want to endorse everything that Bill Leonard said about the overemphasis on election night coverage and on the convention coverage. It occurred to me, as he was giving us that little budget rundown, that $15 million essentially on one night and four days of coverage is the same amount of money I had available for the entire year 1980 for the *Chicago Sun Times*, the whole editorial budget for one year, and that's a lot of money.

But going beyond that, one of things that I had been thinking about these last two days of this meeting is that many of the things that impinge upon the way we do our job really are not susceptible to any control by us, and they are issues that I think have to be considered. One is the increasing length of the presidential election campaign. We heard reference to the fact that it is now a permanent thing, four years long.

I think that has an overriding effect on some of the things that we have to do as a result, and really that is something that we cannot affect in any way. We can't take it upon ourselves in this room to say that henceforth the election campaign should be cut to six weeks, à la the United Kingdom, and let it go at that. That is a decision that has to be made by a group or bunch of people that is far larger than us.

The other thing that only today have we begun to talk about a little bit more coherently, which I am really personally just very worried about, is the whole matter of political commercials and the effects that they are going to have on the electoral process. Once again, that is not anything that we in this room can agree to abolish and then say to the American public, "Henceforth there will be no political commercials." But I sure think that problem should be tackled and somebody should say that henceforth there should be no more thirty-second or one-minute political commercials or even five-minute political commercials. I think that the whole idea of just allowing the candidates to package their message in that way is wrong.

Similarly, debates are an extremely important part of the way television covers the campaign; I think that there should be some kind of mechanism developed for a permanent debating structure so that there is not this kind of minuet every four years in which terms are worked out so that one candidate or the other is going to have an advantage. If there is a mechanism for three debates an election or five debates an election or whatever it's going to be on a certain set schedule, then that kind of advantage will not accrue to a Ronald Reagan or a Jimmy Carter.

Also, I think we need a mechanism in our electoral process for ensuring the complete airing of minority views. I don't think that there was enough attention devoted at this meeting to the John Anderson problem in the general election and the exclusion of John Anderson from the debate. Granted that Anderson might not have been a viable candidate and was not a viable candidate in 1980, but we should not be so short-sighted in our view as to exclude the possibility that what might be happening in 1980 could conceivably come to fruition in 1984 or 1988 or even 1992, and we have to keep that very much in mind.

One other thing that impinges on the whole electoral process and on us is the increasing amount of money being spent, and I don't think that all of the campaign spending laws and rules and regulations that we now have in place really handled that problem as well as it should be handled. The rise of the political action committees and the amount of money that they can spread around is a problem that has to be dealt with; and once again, it is a problem that impinges on the media, on how the media does its job.

I think somehow we need a wider forum to deal with those kinds of things.

One thing that can be discussed in this kind of forum, but I don't think really was discussed satisfactorily enough, was the question of the public opinion polls, the exit polls, and the influence that that could potentially have on elections that are not yet completed when the polls aren't closed.

Dot Ridings

I'm not a good one to give an overview of a conference like this because while I'm a journalist, I have never had anything to do with television, and I found this a perfectly fascinating weekend to learn a lot.

I was particularly heartened to hear Bill Leonard say what he said about the cost of election night coverage. In some humor, he responded to a comment I made about exit polls and projections as, you know, you think that exit polls and projections cause cancer. I would be tempted, I think, in response to that, to say that quite seriously we do have a cancerous kind of problem on a public policy issue of how exit polls and projections do affect the political process.

The only other thing I would like to comment on is the other area for which I think I was invited to participate, and that's the subject of presidential debates. Elizabeth Drew raised today the questions that are the very real ones to me about the role of the candidates in determining format, panel or no panel, how many there will be.

As you probably know, very little of it in 1980 went the way that the league wanted it to go, and we are very concerned about that.

Richard Salant

There are a great many things I want to say. But I can't do justice to some of the concerns that I have, that I don't think were explicitly addressed, that really underlie many of the problems that we now have and are going to get worse.

Just let me name two. One Bill Leonard touched on. There is a very serious, a very, very serious threat to our performance of the journalistic function by the new emphasis, much greater than it is has ever been before, on a word that I haven't even heard said at this meeting. We called it "circulation." It's ratings.

And when they start fiddle-faddling with one of the best network news broadcasts, the CBS Morning News, Monday through Friday, so it is no longer a news broadcast or a hard-news broadcast, only because of ratings, I'm very worried.

And then there is one other issue, which is going to offend many of my colleagues here: the new role of agents, the agents for what we now call stars and who are journalists. Look, let them make as much money as they can, that's fine. It breaks my heart that they should get so much more money than my children's teachers, but I don't know what I can do about that.

But the agents are now beginning to do what has happened in entertainment; they are taking over control of assignments and taking over control of who does what. The management functions are beginning, by force of circumstances, to be shared with people who aren't even in the organization.

Finally, as we look down the road and we see all these new technologies, and the data retrieval and the interactive stuff, people will only call up the information in which they are already interested. You are going to have smaller and smaller groups knowing more and more about less and less; and what makes our political system work is at least some measure of a common data base. Call it homogenization, call it any nasty word you need, we have got to have it.

Jonathan Moore

We got some really good enlightenment, some good discourses, some good insights out on the table, and yet there was a recurrent reluctance to admit and share all that we knew, as we discussed certain issues.

I think on our part, the organizers of the conference, if we have arrogance, it is not that we want to tell somebody what their problems are, let alone tell them what the solutions are; it is that we may tend to be more idealistic about you than we have any right to.

After all, if one cares about this political process the way all of us do, one tends to sympathize with and count on the people who have the most power and have the most valuable role to play, in hopes that they, despite the good job that they are doing, will do an even better job.

I think the best measure of a willingness toward self-analysis and toward measuring the consequences of our actions on others in a shared pluralistic system of many actors is the sponsorship of this conference by the people in the networks, who, with our modest help, put it together.

Appendix: Conference Moderators, Participants/Observers, Committee, and Staff

Moderators

Floyd Abrams, Partner, Cahill, Gordon and Reindel

Tyrone Brown, Former Commissioner, Federal Communications Commission; Member, Steptoe & Johnson

Anthony Lewis, Correspondent, *New York Times*

Ithiel DeSola Pool, Professor of Political Science and Director of the Research Program on Communications Policy, Massachusetts Institute of Technology

Benno C. Schmidt, Jr., Professor of Law, Columbia Law School

Participants/Observers

Graham T. Allison, Jr., Dean and Professor, John F. Kennedy School of Government

Joseph Angotti, Executive Producer, NBC News

Roone Arledge, President, ABC News and Sports

F. Christopher Arterton, Associate Professor of Political Science, Yale University

Ben H. Bagdikian, Professor, Graduate School of Journalism, University of California at Berkeley

Tom Brokaw, News Correspondent, NBC News

Ronald H. Brown, Deputy Chairman, Democratic National Committee; Partner, Patton, Boggs & Blow

Harold Bruno, Jr., Director of Political Coverage, ABC News

Adam Clymer, Political Correspondent, *New York Times*

Les Crystal, Senior Executive Producer, Political Coverage and Special Programs, NBC News

John D. Deardourff, Chairman of the Board, Bailey, Deardourff and Associates

Edwin Diamond, Editorial Director, *Ad Week*

Elizabeth Drew, Journalist

David L. Garth, President, Garth Group

Henry Geller, Director, Washington Center for Public Policy Research

David R. Gergen, Assistant to the President for Communications, The White House

Alan Gerson, Vice-President, Law and Broadcast Administration, NBC News

Jeffrey Gralnick, Vice-President and Executive Producer, Special Events, ABC News

Mimi Gurbst, Associate Producer, ABC News

Betty Hudson, Vice-President, Corporate Relations, NBC Inc.

W. Hamilton Jordan, Distinguished Visiting Fellow, Emory University

Jack Kiermaier, Vice-President, Public Affairs, CBS Inc.

Ernest Leiser, Vice-President and Special Assistant to the President, CBS News

William Leonard, President, CBS News

Martin Linsky, Assistant Director, Institute of Politics

Stuart Loory, Vice-President and Managing Editor, Cable News Network

Robert MacNeil, Executive Editor, The MacNeil-Lehrer Report

Mary McInnis, Assistant General Counsel, CBS Inc.

Newton N. Minow, Former Chairman of the Federal Communications Commission; Partner, Sidley and Austin

Warren Mitofsky, Director, Election/Survey Unit, CBS News

Nicholas T. Mitropoulos, Assistant Director, Institute of Politics

Jonathan Moore, Director, Institute of Politics

Jo Moring, Vice-President, Radio News, NBC News

Bruce Morton, Correspondent, CBS News

Roger Mudd, Chief Washington Correspondent, NBC News

Robert J. Murphy, Director of News Coverage, ABC News

Richard E. Neustadt, Professor of Public Administration, John F. Kennedy School of Government

Richard M. Neustadt, Kirkland & Ellis

David R. Obey, Member of U.S. House of Representatives (D-Wisconsin)

Anthony Oettinger, Chairman and Professor, Program on Information Resources Policy

Stan Opotowsky, Director of Political Operations, ABC News

Gary Orren, Associate Professor of Public Policy, John F. Kennedy School of Government

Martin Plissner, Political Director, CBS News

Gerald Rafshoon, President, Rafshoon Communications

George Reedy, Nieman Professor of Journalism, Marquette University

Frank Reynolds, Chief Anchor, World News Tonight, ABC News

Joan Richman, Vice-President and Director of Special Events, CBS News

Dot Ridings, First Vice-President and Communications Chair, League of Women Voters of the United States

Michael J. Robinson, Director, Media Analysis Project, George Washington University

Richard S. Salant, Former President, CBS News

Irwin Segelstein, Vice-Chairman of the Board, NBC Inc.

Stephen A. Sharp, General Counsel; Federal Communications Commission

William Small, President, NBC News

Frank Stanton, Retired President, CBS Inc.

James C. Thomson, Jr., Curator, Nieman Foundation

Richard Wald, Senior Vice-President, ABC News

John William Ward, President-Elect, American Council of Learned Societies

George Watson, Vice-President, ABC News

David Webster, U.S. Director, British Broadcasting Corporation

Roy Wetzel, General Manager, Elections and Polling, NBC News

Richard B. Wirthlin, President, Decision/Making/Information

Lewis Wolfson, Professor of Communication, School of Communication, American University

Judy Woodruff, White House Correspondent, NBC News

C. Robert Zelnick, Deputy Bureau Chief, Washington Bureau, ABC News

Committee

Mimi Gurbst, ABC

Jack Kiermaier, CBS

Betty Hudson, NBC

Martin Linsky, Institute of Politics

Staff

Jonathan Moore, Director, Institute of Politics

Thomas G. White, Conference Coordinator

Tony Butler

Michael Cornfield

Brian Gallogly

Larry Goldberg

Jane Markham

Nicholas Mitropoulos

Evelyn Perez

Betsy Pleasants

Penelope Wells

Bibliography

If the three-day session transcribed in this volume marked an intersection for the organized lives of electronic journalists, communications lawyers, social scientists, campaign veterans, and other public professionals, then this bibliography aims to lead readers beyond that intersection in four directions: back through the histories of the mass medium and the quadrennial events it covers and forward through the speculative avenues of criticism on television and national politics.

The published writings that sprawl outward from the conference crossroads tend to be highly individualistic and timebound. Every author, it seems, brings to the subject an up-to-the-minute distillation of political preferences, viewing tastes, and vocational predilections. No two see eye to eye on what the problems are or where they lie at any given time—and there is no "given time" because candidates, issues, election regulations, news formats, reporters, and technologies change constantly. This makes generalized knowledge hard to acquire. Much of the literature justifies the suspicion that this topic will be forever trapped in a kaleidoscope of shifting personal opinions and ephemeral priorities. But this state of relativism has inspired some lively and significant commentary.

Some observations and judgments have proven better than others, less susceptible to tomorrow's erosions of today's prevalent concerns. A few people have accumulated more telling evidence or experience and also found the right words to describe and analyze them. Examples of their work are listed below.

Abel, Elie, ed. *What's News*. San Francisco: Institute for Contemporary Studies, 1981. Essays by E.J. Epstein, J. Hulteng, and G. Comstock especially recommended in this interdisciplinary survey of media issues.

Adams, William, and Schreibman, Fay, eds. *Television Network News*. Washington, D.C.: George Washington University, 1978. The best available guide to social-science research on television in America. Extensive lists of scholarly articles and essays on how the fields of inquiry have been divided.

Adler, Richard, ed. *Television As A Social Force*. New York: Praeger, 1975. Papers for a Aspen Institute conference. Of particular interest

This bibliography was prepared by Michael Cornfield, who is completing a doctoral dissertation on American political journalism in the Department of Government at Harvard University.

are contributions by Paul Weaver, Michael Robinson, and David Littlejohn.

Agranoff, Robert. "Campaign Media in the Age of Television." In *The New Style in Election Campaigns*, edited by Robert Agranoff. Rockleigh, N.J.: Holbrook Press, 1976. A dated but well-organized discussion of technological changes and the techniques prevalent in their use.

Annals of the American Academy of Political and Social Science, September 1976. A volume devoted to the topic, with key articles by Michael Petrick on regulatory issues and Joseph Napolitan on costs and benefits of various campaign strategies.

Asher, Herbert. *Presidential Elections and American Politics*, 1980 Edition. Homewood, Ill.: Dorsey Press. The best overview of conflicts as they surface at the primary, convention, final, and election-day stages, covering controversies from 1952 to 1976. Pages 249–268 provide the key discussions.

Barber, James David, ed. *Choosing the President*. Englewood Cliffs, N.J.: American Assembly/Prentice-Hall, 1974. Notable for an essay by Murray Edelman that explores how different audiences get different messages about politics through television.

Barber, James David, ed. *Race for the Presidency*: *The Media and the Nominating Process*. Englewood Cliffs, N.J.: Prentice-Hall, 1978. The two opening essays by Christopher Arterton are excellent political-science analyses: systematic, precise, documented.

Beer, Samuel. "Government and Politics: An Imbalance." *Center Magazine*, March/April 1974, pp. 10–22. What national political parties do. What happens to public affairs when they don't. A lucid philosophical essay.

Benjamin, Gerald, ed. *The Communications Revolution in Politics*. New York: Academy of Political Science, 1982. Brief, wide-ranging articles on the gamut of electronic media and their applications in politics. See especially the pieces by Barnouw, Patterson, Bieder, Everson, and Roll. (Joan Bieder's essay includes a description of the conference transcribed in this book.)

Broder, David. "Political Reporters in Presidential Politics." *The Washington Monthly*, February 1969, pp. 20–33. Still the most penetrating and concise description of what the pack does.

Brotman, Stuart N. "New Campaigning for the New Media," and Dodge, Charles S. "FCC Watch," *Campaigns and Elections*, Fall 1981, pp. 32–34 and 49–52. Brief updates on current and future regulatory issues. The magazine is a new resource for students of the subject.

"Modern Technology: Problem or Opportunity?" *Daedalus*, Winter 1980. Highly recommended are the opening symposium; an essay by Harvey

Brooks that compares society's choice of appropriate technologies to the evolutionary process of natural selection; and Langdon Winner's answer to the question he poses in his essay's title, "Do Artifacts Have Politics?"

Diamond, Edwin. *The Tin Kazoo; Good News, Bad News; Sign Off: The Last Days of Television*. Cambridge, Mass.: M.I.T. Press, 1975, 1978, 1982. Lively, often incisive looks at various topics in media criticism by a journalist turned professional student of the subject.

Drew, Elizabeth. *American Journal: The Events of 1976; and Portrait of an Election: The 1980 Presidential Election*. New York: Random House, 1977; New York: Simon and Schuster, 1981. Unique among her peers, Elizabeth Drew actually keeps a public *journal*, interweaving interviews, observations, memo excerpts, and understated commentary. The best source for a sense of the rhythms of the campaign process.

Friendly, Fred. *The Good Guys, The Bad Guys, and the First Amendment*. New York: Vintage/Random House, 1976. About *Red Lion*, the landmark case involving the fairness doctrine and the First Amendment, with some stimulating proposals about how to resolve some enduring regulatory issues.

Gans, Herbert. *Deciding What's News*. New York: Pantheon, 1978. Gans's thick prose obscures an important, creative discussion of the "enduring values" inherent to the network news (and the news weeklies).

Graber, Doris. "Mass Media and American Politics." Washington, D.C.: *Congressional Quarterly*, 1980. Broad treatment of the impact of one upon the other. Includes the uninspired but firmly based results of her survey of twenty newspapers and the three networks as they covered the last month of the 1968, 1972, and 1976 elections.

Greenfield, Jeff. *Playing to Win*. New York: Simon and Schuster, 1980. A breezy, anecdotal, consistently bright look at campaigning. Greenfield likes to knock down straw men, but the field seems populated with them, so it's a valuable exercise.

Greenfield, Jeff. *The Real Campaign*. New York: Summit Books, 1982. Another breezy, anecdotal volume debunking the conventional wisdom. This one is about the impact, or more accurately, the lack of impact of the media on the 1980 presidential election.

Hodgson, Godfrey. *America in Our Time*. New York: Vintage, 1978. A well-researched, cogent, and remarkably comprehensive history of post-World War II America, with emphasis on the 1960s and 1970s. Chapters 7 and 19 offer as good an overview of the topics discussed in this volume as has been written.

Jensen, Richard. "Armies, Admen, and Campaigners." *The History Teacher*, January 1969, pp. 33–45. (Also reprised in *Public Opinion*, September/

October, 1980.) Most ingenious classificatory approach to presidential elections in terms of how campaigns conceive of their mission.

Lang, K., and Lang, G.E. *Politics and Television*. Chicago, Ill.: Quadrangle, 1968. The top book on the subject also happens to be the oldest; this volume assembles the Langs's studies of the 1950s and early 1960s. Yet precisely because they look at the early years, their frameworks and observations have a depth not matched since TV became omnipresent.

Lipset, Seymour Martin, ed. *Politics and the Social Sciences*. New York: Oxford, 1969. How scholars approach the big, bad world. Of particular use is Richard Jensen's contribution, a history of "American Election Analysis," that ranges from 1787 to the post-World War II period, pp. 226–243.

MacNeil, Robert. *The People Machine*. New York: Harper and Row, 1968. "Electronic Schizophrenia: Does TV Alienate Voters." *Politeia*, Summer 1972. Confessions of a troubled television newscaster.

Moore, Jonathan, ed. *The Campaign for President: 1980 in Retrospect*. Cambridge, Mass.: Ballinger, 1981. A volume in which both sides are presented and indeed become many sides of a story. The "Rashomon" approach to political narrative gives media and campaign participants equal time.

Ranney, Austin, ed. *The Past and Future of Presidential Debates*. Washington, D.C.: American Enterprise Institute, 1978. The best contribution is by Jack Germond and Jules Witcover, pp. 191–205.

Rosenthal, Jack. "Being There." *New York Times* Editorial Notebook, July 22, 1980. The Peter Sellers film inspires an intelligent, witty essay with a unique observation: that you can not watch a convention from the floor any more.

Saldich, Anne Rawley. *Electronic Democracy*. New York: Praeger, 1979. Television as the "great democratizer," a good that has yet to be maximized. (For the counterargument, see Walzer, below.)

Sennett, Richard. *The Fall of Public Man*. New York: Vintage, 1978. A sweeping complex indictment of modern life as held against Paris and London of centuries past. The dangers of electronic intimacy and the idea of charisma (from Max Weber and Sigmund Freud to Richard Nixon and Bruce Springsteen) are discussed.

Shales, Tom. "Petty for Teddy." *Washington Post*, January 30, 1980. Also, Walsh, Edward. "Through the Eyes of a Needler." *Washington Post*, February 16, 1980, and Clark, Blair. "Notes on a No-Win Campaign." *Columbia Journalism Review*, September/October 1980, pp. 36–41. Three looks at what, if anything, television did to the presidential candidacy of Senator Edward M. Kennedy in early 1980.

Sigal, Leon. "Newsmen and Campaigners." *Political Science Quarterly*, Fall 1978, pp. 465–470. How and why each party to the process tends to overrate the contribution of the other. Argues that media people do not winnow out aspirants so much as they winnow in the early-primary victors.

Small, William J. *Political Power and the Press*. New York: Norton, 1972. A network-news executive comes to the defense of his industry.

Smith, Anthony, ed. *Television and Political Life: Studies in Six European Countries*. New York: Saint Martin's Press, 1979. A generally well-written anthology, valuable here as an aid to determining what effects inhere to the technology of TV as opposed to what effects stem from our peculiar political system and culture.

Tuchman, Gaye. *Making News*. New York: Free Press, 1978. Tuchman takes commonly used terms from journalism such as *hard news* and defines them so she can build a framework that journalists implicitly rely on when they attempt to represent social reality through words, sounds, and images. If that seems convoluted and overcomplicated, so will the book. But Tuchman, like Gans, is very smart and has some interesting observations on the way journalists treated the women's movement.

U.S. House of Representatives, Subcommittee on Communications. *Options Papers*, May 1977, 95th Congress, First Session. This Congress marked the beginning of this subcommittee's effort to look at the entire ball of wax, toward a systematic revamping of the communications act of 1934. This volume contains a wide array of possible legal steps in virtually every issue pertinent to the mass-communications industry. Of particular relevance to the conference are papers on cable television and on telecommunications regulation.

Walzer, Michael. "Democracy vs. Elections." *The New Republic*, January 3 and 10, 1981, pp. 17–19. A tightly reasoned case against the primaries and television as an appropriate forum for politics. He recognizes that this constitutes a blow against direct democracy, but he nevertheless wants less of it in the presidential selection process. (See Ranney, *The Past and Future of Presidential Debates*.)

Weaver, Paul. "Captives of Melodrama." *The New York Times Magazine*, August 29, 1976, pp. 6, 48–57. Weaver reviews the flow of the story as TV news depicted the 1976 primaries. He finds a Teddy White approach run rampant, wherein the people lift one of their own to the highest office in the land after a series of grueling tests.

Wolfinger, Raymond, and Linquitti, Peter. "Tuning in and Turning Out." *Public Opinion*, February/March 1981, pp. 56–60. A review of the studies and a discussion of the issues surrounding TV reporting East Coast election results before the West Coast polls have closed.

Finally, for a more exhaustive bibliography see:

Harrell, Karen F. "The Role of Television in U.S. Politics and Government, 1961–1981." Vance Bibliographies, P.O. Box 229, Monticello, IL 61856. ($2.00)

About the Editor

Martin Linsky is the assistant director of the Institute of Politics, Harvard University, where he is directing a three-year study of how the press affects federal policymaking. He teaches courses on ethics of the media and legislative behavior at the John F. Kennedy School of Government, Harvard University. Mr. Linsky's career as a journalist includes five years as editor of *The Real Paper* in Boston and two years as an editorial writer for the *Boston Globe*. From 1967 to 1972 he served as a member of the Massachusetts House of Representatives. He was educated at Williams College and Harvard Law School. His articles and commentary have been published in the *Wall Street Journal*, the *New Republic*, and *The Bulletin* of the American Society of Newspaper Editors, among many other publications.